Signs of Civilisation

Bård Borch Michalsen is the author of several books about communication, language and writing, including *Comma*, published in Norway in 2014. Having worked for many years as a journalist and newspaper editor, he is now an associate professor at the Arctic University of Norway where he teaches communication and project management.

BÅRD BORCH MICHALSEN

Signs of Civilisation

How punctuation changed history

Translated from the Norwegian
by Christine Rae Walter

SCEPTRE

First published in Great Britain in 2019 by Sceptre
An Imprint of Hodder & Stoughton
An Hachette UK company

This paperback edition published in 2020

1

First published in Norwegian as *Tegn til Sivilisasjon* by Spartacus in 2019
Translation from Norwegian by Christine Rae Walter in association
with First Edition Translations Ltd, Cambridge, UK

The publication of this translation has been made possible through
the financial support of NORLA, Norwegian Literature Abroad

A CIP catalogue record for this title is available from the British Library

Paperback ISBN 9781529326710
Hardback ISBN 9781529326734
eBook ISBN 9781529326727

Contents

Introduction

Once upon a time we were apes, and back then we shared a favourite occupation: we scratched each other's backs. Occasionally this habit may be due to vermin or uncleanliness, but the apes in some tribes spend 20 per cent of their waking hours scratching each other's backs. What can be the reason for this?

The evolutionary psychologist Robin Dunbar found the answer: apes cannot speak, so they have to express themselves in other ways. That is where scratching comes in. When one ape scratches another's back, it is also saying, 'I like you.' The ape that is being scratched feels relaxed and secure – quite simply, slightly euphoric.

The apes that have not developed into humans are still apes. If they had been able to speak or write they would have asked what happened to those of us who became human. How have we managed to go so much further than they have? We know the answer: we learned to speak. That was a big step. Later we realised that it might be a good idea to write down our thoughts, opinions, ideas, observations, reflections, exclamations and questions. Then we progressed much further.

The apes, poor things, are still sitting up in the trees scratching each other's backs to say *I like you*. We humans developed further, with the written language as the powerful driving force. The written word became truly refined 500 years ago. That was when punctuation entered the system and became standardised. This was not in order to make writing more difficult but to make reading easier, and today punctuation marks still ensure that words work effectively.

But are we nevertheless on our way back to the way apes communicate? Emojis are taking over written communication, and what do we do in order to express friendship ourselves? We often make do with a ☺ or a 😊

Fastidious puritans with boxes full of red pens dislike changes to language that have taken place since they left school. The book you are now reading is written from the standpoint that language inevitably changes, and that this also applies to the written language. We use different words, acquire new words, combine words in sentences in new ways – and make adjustments to the way we punctuate. And we use the language in new channels, new situations and new genres. So language is a living organism that adapts to its times and comes into existence as we speak and write.

That is how things are: clever minds have contributed to the invention of ways of writing that ensure that what we write is understood quickly, efficiently and correctly by readers. The full stop, comma, exclamation mark and question mark are examples of this kind of linguistic aid. The way these marks are used also changes over the centuries. However, there is no reason to reject the basic principles of punctuation that have made the written word a superior means of communication for 500 years.

The purpose of this book is to sweep through the part of European cultural history that deals with the most important punctuation marks. Welcome to the story of signs of civilisation!

Harstad, June 2019
Bård Borch Michalsen

PART I

1494: It Was Finished

The World Before Writing

We managed very well without being able to write or speak but, as we know, once we become accustomed to something that we experience as making life easier, a real step forward, we are not keen to have it taken away from us again. Can you imagine life without smartphones, water closets and mains electricity? That is how it used to be with speech.

In the beginning, it was not the word, but when we first began to use our mouths for something more than eating and biting, we discovered the great advantages that came with the new development. We could report on threats of danger, we could tell spicy stories about the escapades of our neighbours in a strange tribe. We could also discuss how we would organise the next day's hunting.

Who was the first person to talk, around 50,000 years ago? Nobody knows. And it is a nonsensical question anyway, as there is no point in being the only person in the world who can talk. We carry on our inner dialogue perfectly well without using our voices; we need speech when we want to be social – and humans are social beings.

Learning to talk was useful, practical and enjoyable. We made good use of the new opportunities. We had already stood up on two legs and begun to walk and run, which gave us an invaluable advantage in the competition with the animals that surrounded us. When people who could run also started to use their mouths to express their thoughts, we soon became superior to all the other species. None could reach a distant goal faster than we could, and because we could talk as we ran, we could also exchange experiences, tell others about dangers along the way, report on handy short-cuts and agree meeting places – and gossip about the people we had seen embracing among the trees where they thought no one could see them. When humans began to talk, we must also have used speech to gossip about anything and everything.

Other species before us had constructed something that could, with a small stretch of the imagination, be called a language but in most cases with sounds that were not articulated. Human speech soon developed into something much more advanced. In his book *Sapiens*, Yuval Noah Harari emphasises the fact that it was the ability to talk about what does not exist for our physical senses that became the truly unique feature of our language: 'As far as we know, only Sapiens can talk about entire kinds of entities that they have never seen, touched or smelled.' He shows how legends, myths, gods and religions arose as a result of the cognitive revolution, an important element of which was innovative speech.

6,000 Years of the History of Writing

However, man cannot live on religion alone. We also need bread, and what would be the best possible way to organise a more advanced system of cooperation, buying and selling? Increased trade brought with it a need to pin down arrangements, obligations and debts in something more durable than verbal agreements. As a result, some 3,500 years before the common era, some bright sparks in Mesopotamia made marks representing words and objects – the first written language! Or was it the first? Historians are unsure, but there are good grounds for believing that written language also came into existence at around the same time in China and Egypt.

The quantum leap made by Semitic peoples near the eastern shores of the Mediterranean was the transition to a system in which the characters no longer depicted objects but instead represented sounds. The alphabet arrived later. That was another big step, both for those who came up with the idea and for humanity in general. According to the media sociologist Manuel Castells, the alphabet is the indispensable infrastructure for cumulative, knowledge-based communication and the basis for western philosophy and science.

The alphabet made it possible to manage with fewer characters (now known as letters). The Semitic alphabet was the first to appear, but it contained only consonants. The Greeks took the next giant step by adding vowels. This also enabled us to read and write words we did not know, including words in foreign languages. The American professor Walter J. Ong devoted his life to researching the connection between language and our ability to think. In his book *Orality and Literacy* he wrote that it was this alphabet that gave Greek culture the upper hand in antiquity. Adding vowels democratised the written language; more and more people were able to read and write. Neurolinguistic studies suggest that a phonetic alphabet with vowels supports analytical, abstract thought. The Roman alphabet evolved from the Greek alphabet, via the alphabet of the Etruscans, who ruled over parts of Italy before the rise of Rome. The Roman alphabet is now the most commonly used in the world.

People found it expedient to begin to write. This was clever, correct thinking. Later, improvements occurred in the language system that enabled us to convey more and to do so with increasing speed and accuracy. The book you are now reading considers punctuation to be the finishing touch to the written languages in Europe; like dotting the i's and crossing the t's, it is the icing on the cake. Punctuation is the system and conventions that give letters and words greater precision and depth, colour and feeling, tone and rhythm. Indeed, the consequences are even more dramatic than this. Punctuation is not merely an important part of our language code; an advanced punctuation system has been nothing less than one of the driving forces in the development of our entire western civilisation.

The first punctuation marks were introduced 2,200 years ago in the ancient cultural capital of Alexandria. The marks were tiny and they were soon dropped by the civilisations surrounding the Mediterranean Sea. The more difficult it was to read, the greater the power of the few who had mastered the art. However, the marks were reinvented and during the Middle Ages many people in Europe realised that, if written languages were to achieve their full potential, they would need to be modernised. Spain, Germany and Ireland reinvented and improved a system of punctuation, thus preparing the ground for the Italian humanists.

A Motor For Our Civilisation

When Yuval Noah Harari in *Sapiens* sought to understand the unique development of the human race, he found two answers. The first was our ability to create imaginary systems of organisation, such as religion or limited companies. The second was written language. In his view, these two inventions filled the gaps in our biological inheritance. Lars Tvede came to the same conclusion in his book *The Creative Society*: Language codes are a prerequisite for successful civilisations. In his hefty standard work *The History and Power of Writing*, Henri-Jean Martin stresses the fact that the foundation of written language coincided with the beginnings of great civilisations, growth, prosperity and increasing communication.

Written language has indisputably been a condition for the growth and advance of civilisations, and this could not have happened without the involvement of commas, question marks and other punctuation marks. The development of punctuation that culminated 500 years ago was essential for progress towards European civilisation. Andrew Reamer of George Washington University wanted to collate the findings of all the research on the effect of technological inventions on economic growth. The innovations to which he draws particular attention are mathematics, critical thinking, methodical research and writing. He refers firstly to the opportunities for growth in trade and communication provided by the first written languages 5,000 years ago, but considers that the great revolution came about through changes in the way text was organised, for example the introduction of spaces between the words and punctuation. These innovations paved the way for silent reading, which allowed the reader to absorb the meaning of the text rapidly and efficiently. Standardised punctuation and other minor changes to the conventions of writing interacted with a truly major innovation – the invention of printing. The manuscript culture was on its way to becoming history.

Printed books were a gift for silent reading. Each one of us could establish a personal and private relationship with God, without the interference of his representatives on earth. Inspired by the wine presses of antiquity, Johannes Gutenberg developed the first printing press, and print shops soon appeared throughout central Europe. The art of printing was praised as a spectacular and truly earth-shaking innovation – and with good reason. Yet at the same time, printed books would have been completely unreadable, if the text had looked the same as it had until the late Middle Ages, namely like this: IFTHETEXTHADAPPEAREDASITHADDONE UNTILTHELATEMIDDLEAGES.

Visually, books needed to be laid out in a way that made them accessible; there had to be agreement on conventions for punctuation that allowed everyone to unravel the meaning behind the words. A language system in which each individual had his or her own rules for spelling, grammar and punctuation would have impeded the development that we now know happened. The modernisation of typography and punctuation is a less obvious innovation than the invention of a physical machine, but it was nonetheless a crucial requirement in order for the products of that machine to be significant. The grammar, punctuation and visual presentation of the text are what we now call software. Without it, the hardware is no more than dead metal.

The innovation gathered speed in sixteenth-century Europe. Innovation and creativity require individual thought that is independent of what authorities might think is true or valuable. The silent reading that had become established made such individual thought possible. The text no longer had to pass through the ears but through the eyes. However, for silent reading it was essential for the text to appear in a different way from previously, with spaces between the words and a fixed system of punctuation. So punctuation was not merely a result of this development but one of the reasons why it was possible for efficient reading to come into being. A common language standard, together with other factors such as exploration, migration and decentralisation, was a key element in a powerful evolutionary impulse that, 500 years ago, started a chain reaction of fast-moving processes. Standardised punctuation is an essential thread woven into the fabric of sixteenth-century Europe, which underwent a sensational technological, economic and cultural development. Lars Tvede summed up this development as follows:

- *The Renaissance*, which promoted artistic activity, humanism, individualism, empirical experiment and creativity.
- *The Enlightenment*, with ideals such as freedom, democracy, religious tolerance, a constitutional state, rationalism and sound reason.
- *The Age of Discovery*.
- *The Reformation*.
- *The Scientific Revolution*.
- *The Industrial Revolution*, when the introduction of machines and mass production led to an explosion of prosperity, urbanisation and cultural upheavals.

Could the French philosopher Descartes (1596–1650) have anything to add here? Nowadays people rarely chat about him over lunch, except possibly in corners where philosophers meet to dine. Nevertheless, there is one question we recognise from television quiz programmes: 'Who is famous for the saying "I think, therefore I am"?' That is Descartes and his thinking man – who is also a writing man! When he has thought, and while he is thinking, he writes, and thus confirms that he thinks. In *Orality and Literacy*, Walter J. Ong stresses the fact that written language is absolutely essential for advanced thinking. Oral culture is not well suited to such phenomena as geometrical figures, abstract thought, logical argument and definitions. These things are not produced by thought alone but through thoughts that are reasoned out and elaborated in text. Descartes might just as well have written: *I write, therefore I am.*

And yes, there has to be a comma in this sentence. Correct punctuation in the right place is worth its weight in gold.

The Greeks Had a Word For It

FORTHEFIRSTMILLENNIATEXTSWERE
WRITTENWITHOUTSPACESANDWITHOUT
PUNCTUATIONTHETEXTSRANFROMLEFTTO
RIGHTORFROMRIGHTTOLEFTANDTHEYWERE
WRITTENUSINGONLYCAPITALLETTERS

The only thing that was reminiscent of punctuation was the long *paragraphos*, a horizontal line that was inserted to mark the beginning or end of a sentence or to indicate that a different character was speaking in a drama. Texts were written as *scriptio continua*, without spaces between the words, and they were difficult to access even for the few who were able to read. There was no division into paragraphs, NOPUNCTUATIONANDEVERYTHINGWASIN CAPITALS

A reader could not begin to understand what was written until the text had been read aloud several times. No one considered the idea that the text could be read silently; it was written to be read aloud as a representation of the spoken word, not as something that could be read noiselessly. At that time, writing was not an independent, paying activity that established its own identity but merely a record of words spoken in poetry, debates or dialogues. Positive changes did not begin to take place until a few centuries before the birth of Christ.

Aristophanes: The forgotten innovator

Outside the Bibliotheca Alexandrina there is now a modest column just by the coffee bar where students from all over the world meet between lectures. The column is said to originate in the library of the ancient Mediterranean city of Alexandria, just a few hundred metres from the place where the new library was built in 2003. The modern library was designed by the Norwegian architectural consortium Snøhetta. It was built to be Egypt's window on the world and the world's window to Egypt, but the ambitions did not stop there. When the library was to be opened, the librarian, Ismail Serageldin, referred to the legacy from the ancient library, which he hoped would now be rediscovered. The Alexandria library is majestic and monumental, and a space not only for books but also for research, teaching and seminars.

The Macedonian Alexander the Great was aged only twenty-five in 332 BC when he conquered the city that was to bear his name from that time on. Alexander died a few years later, and not long afterwards a Greek royal house took over power in the city. The Ptolemaic dynasty, as it was known, initiated a golden age of Greek culture that lasted several hundred years, in which the original Hellas was no longer the most important element. During this period of Hellenistic culture the political, economic and cultural focus moved to Alexandria. The Ptolemaic dynasty's large income from natural resources such as papyrus was used not least for the building of the centre of learning, the Museion, with its famous library, the purpose of which was to collect everything that had been written in Greek. Books were brought in from the whole of the Hellenistic world, and the library also sent its employees further afield to track down books. The librarians were interested in everything, though texts about language and literature were the first priority. Historians have suggested that, at its peak, the library may have contained almost 500,000 scrolls.

Alexandria was the cultural and intellectual centre of the ancient world and a place where ideas from Asia and Europe could meet. Academic stars appeared and were nurtured in the fields of literature, medicine, astronomy, geometry and mathematics. The most famous of them is possibly Archimedes, who discovered the principle of the buoyancy of a body in water.

The library was also famous for its many talented librarians. One of these was Eratosthenes. As well as looking after the books, he was interested in geography, mathematics and astronomy and he was the first to determine the circumference of the Earth. Eratosthenes calculated it to be 39,250 km, and this is not far away from what we now know to be correct – 40,075 km. So it is not without reason that he is held up as one of the library's truly great minds. The librarians who followed Eratosthenes are usually mentioned only in passing in descriptions of the library's history.

But not here! We must honour one of them, Aristophanes of Byzantium (257–180 BC), and provide him with the memorial he has not been given in the new Bibliotheca Alexandrina. He is almost unknown there, considered as no more than a side issue. Not even in the innermost offices of the Alexandria Center for Hellenistic Studies is there a trace of chief librarian Aristophanes and his contribution to our punctuation system. There are no researchers sitting absorbed over fragments of worn papyrus scrolls, awed by the use of the colon, no posters praising his contribution to the full stop, not so much as a faded drawing on the wall of the comma he introduced.

If you are already familiar with a man named Aristophanes, the chances are that your acquaintance is not the librarian and grammarian but the comic playwright of the same name.

Even in those days, the production of popular culture brought greater celebrity status than taking the very prerequisites of language a few, indispensable steps further. Of course this is not intended to say anything insulting about the dramatist who wrote such immortal comedies as *Lysistrata*.

However, the hero here is a different Aristophanes. He was aged 60 when he became the head of the library. His ability to attract capable experts is said to have been limited, but be that as it may, what no one can take away from him is the fact that he drew up the world's first punctuation system. In addition, he introduced the use of accents in Greek, which made it easier for those whose mother tongue was not Greek to pronounce the words correctly. Punctuation and diacritical marks were both essentials for a properly functioning written language. Greek is a particularly musical language, writes the Italian author Andrea Marcolongo in *La lingua geniale* (2016). That is why Greek-speakers make particularly good use of accents and punctuation. In that way the rhythm and nuances of intonation were transferred from the spoken language to its reproduction in writing.

In his study in Alexandria, Aristophanes pondered on what might make it easier to read literature from the past and the present. He suggested adopting three signs in order to make it easier to read the enormous quantity of earlier Greek texts that the librarians had been employed to edit and make accessible for posterity. Because it was a matter of preparing the material for the way it was read in the past – reading aloud – the system developed by Aristophanes was a so-called rhetorical system. It cared little for grammar, being exclusively concerned with how pauses could make it easier to present the text orally in a comprehensible way.

Where was it necessary to pause between the pieces of text? Aristophanes' basic idea was to furnish the texts with *distinctiones*, circular signs that were to be placed at different heights according to the importance and length of the pause to be marked. *Comma, colon* and *period* were rhetorical terms for passages that are short, medium-length or long. The terms we still use, such as comma and colon (and in American English, *period* for full stop), were not originally punctuation marks but rather the parts of the text that were to be separated by these markers.

Aristophanes worked with three different marks:

- Highest: *Distinctio*: a final pause after a *period,* where the meaning is complete.
- In the middle: *Media distinctio*: indicates a short pause after a *comma,* or where the meaning is incomplete.
- Low: *Subdistinctio*: indicates a slightly longer pause after a *colon,* or where the sentence is complete but the meaning is not.

Dionysios Thrax (170–90 BC) was born, probably in Alexandria, ten years after Aristophanes' death. Thrax wrote what may have been the first systematic grammar in the western world, and it was used in schools in the Roman Empire for centuries. It was printed for the first time in 1816. The main features of the two points that concern punctuation refer to Aristophanes' system, and the rules match what Thrax defined as the purpose of the grammatical knowledge he wished to convey: to help with the reading aloud of texts as required by the situation, the genre and the contents. He posed the rhetorical question of what distinguishes what we now call a comma from a full stop and provided the answer himself: the comma indicates a short pause and the full stop a long pause.

Aristophanes' punctuation system was simple, but we should not hold that against it. Two of the three marks he introduced are still the most important today – the comma and the full stop. Aristophanes got there first. It required courage, ingenuity and drive to try to change a system that had functioned in its own way for hundreds of years. Aristophanes was daring, capable and willing, and many of the basic ideas behind his punctuation system still apply. Credit and kudos to Aristophanes, who could keep so many balls in the air. In addition to putting forward principles for a functional punctuation system, he edited new, more readable editions of Homer's *Iliad* and *Odyssey*, written 500 years earlier. Aristophanes himself was also a writer, and he had a predilection for unusual and old-fashioned words, which he collected. Unfortunately, little of what he wrote has survived except for fragments quoted by later authors.

The years that followed Aristophanes were not very pleasant in Alexandria. The magnificent library was destroyed a few years after he had written his last full stop. What happened and when is unclear, but it is certain that the library was razed to the ground, possibly as the result of a fire, when Julius Caesar arrived from the west and conquered the city in 47 BC.

The Ptolemaic dynasty, which had made Alexandria into a cultural metropolis, fared little better. Cleopatra, the last of the Ptolemaic rulers, certainly did her best and even a bit extra in order to cling on to power and honour, but the dangerous game she played with Julius Caesar, Mark Antony and others ended in ruin. Historians are still muttering about whether she committed suicide in despair. The Roman conquest meant that Alexandria lost its position as the leading centre of Greco-Egyptian culture; it was downgraded to a provincial town. Nevertheless, the city remained one of the largest in the Roman Empire. The tradition of learning lived on and later made it antiquity's centre of Christian theology.

1,000 Years of Darkness: Oblivion

The centre of power now moved westward from the Hellenistic Empire to Rome. However, the mood here was not conducive to the retention of Aristophanes' punctuation system. The great orator Cicero considered punctuation marks completely unnecessary. All the same, the Romans had inherited from the Etruscans the idea of inserting markers between the words to separate them from one another. These *interpuncts* were used mainly when a text was to be written in a more enduring form, for example, carved on a stone wall: *dona*nobis*pacem* ('give us peace'). Tourists in Rome can still admire inscriptions with such markings on the city's walls and streets.

However, this custom also died out. The Romans were so enthusiastic about classical Greek culture that they also reintroduced the custom of *scriptio continua*, meaning text without spaces between the words, and with no marks to indicate short or slightly longer pauses. Thorough preparations for spoken performances demanded meticulous reading and interpretation. The teachers (*grammatici*) played a key role in this; they taught the pupils through *praelectiones* (lectures) so that they were able to read the text easily and accurately. During this teaching, the teachers or the pupils inserted marks in the text to divide or join up words, and marked long syllables or pauses.

The task of punctuation gradually became professionalised, meaning that selected persons were entrusted with the task of inserting marks in manuscripts to ensure that they were understood in the way the author desired. Manuscripts that were treated in this fashion in the fifth and sixth centuries became known as *codices distincti*. The purpose of the markings was – as in Ancient Greece – to prepare them for flawless spoken performances. Incidences of silent reading were still so rare that they caused raised eyebrows. Christian teachers gradually took over the role of punctuators, and this did not happen purely by chance. The way the Bible was written down and treated was important for understanding. Yet in many of the monasteries where the monks worked on biblical texts and other literary tasks, punctuation disappeared once again. The monks of southern Europe considered that they were such expert readers that inserting punctuation was unnecessary.

Further north there was hope. When Ireland became Christian, the Irish had to learn Latin. Latin was completely foreign to them, so they needed all the help they could get, and it came by boat. In the year AD 405, Saint Jerome (AD 347–420) had presented his complete translation of the Bible from Greek and Hebrew into Latin. Inspired by earlier celebrated orators such as Cicero and Demosthenes, Jerome wrote *per cola et commata*, meaning that, when it suited the reading,

the text continued on a new line.

This made it easier to read.

The Irish monks eagerly took over the method when Saint Jerome's Bible, known as the *Vulgate*, reached the Emerald Isle in the western sea after just 30 years. The monks also made a real attempt to kill off *scriptio continua*. All in all, it is striking that for several hundred years the signs of progress in the written language appeared in monasteries in Ireland – far from the centres of power of mainland Europe.

However, we Scandinavians who live a long way off the European beaten track must also share the blame for the fact that punctuation had to suffer serious setbacks. In AD 568, the Lombards, or Langobardi, conquered the Roman empire. The Long-Beards – the meaning of the tribe's name – came from northern Germany but they were of Scandinavian origin, and at that time people in Scandinavia were not very interested in commas and suchlike; we were mainly preoccupied with satisfying people's primary needs – war and peace and so on.

The invasion hastened the final collapse of the Roman Empire – and thus also the demise of classical culture. Pope Gregory the Great realised that something had to be done quickly in order to avoid a total catastrophe. In AD 590, he had a *Regula pastoralis* drawn up. The text was written in beautiful calligraphy with punctuation – high for short pauses, low for final pauses (which took the form of a comma, as below) – and in such a way that as little interpretation as possible would be left to the reader,

But the age of antiquity was over. The Roman Empire fell, taking punctuation with it.

Developments continued in fits and starts throughout the whole of the Middle Ages. One of the most important drivers of change was people's attitude to the written word. Written language had long been considered a means of capturing the spoken word for subsequent oral communication, but writing now gradually began to be considered as an independent means of bringing information directly to the mind through the eye. Isidore of Seville (AD 560–636) was the first advocate of silent reading. He thought it was a more efficient way of understanding and remembering – and less of a struggle. We can award him a point for this. Isidore was classically educated and classically minded. He was in close contact with monks who had fled to Spain from North Africa, where Islam was expanding. Isidore saw the need for teaching the writings of classical antiquity and this moved him to improve and develop punctuation and other aspects of visual presentation. Isidore's meticulous work influenced punctuation and the craft of writing for many centuries, not only in southern Europe but also in the Anglo-Saxon countries. He was the first person to believe that punctuation could be used syntactically in order to define grammatical units; until then, it had been motivated by the needs of people who were reading aloud.

All the same, reading aloud continued to predominate throughout the medieval period. Silent reading was considered almost suspicious, for who knew what obscenities might be going through the mind of the reader? Some doctors recommended reading aloud as a physical activity on a par with running, while others issued warnings, asserting that silent reading could damage the throat or internal organs.

Exceptionally, a few people in the ancient world are thought to have practised silent reading, if they had good reason to do so. Alexander the Great read a letter from his mother Olympia without using his voice, and Julius Caesar is also said to have been observed silently reading a letter to himself. Could it have been from the beautiful Cleopatra?

In the fourth century the famous theologian Augustine came to Milan. There he paid a visit to Bishop Ambrose, and the visit made Augustine excited. When Ambrose had a text in front of him, he scanned the page with his eyes and his heart sought the meaning, but it all happened without a sound and his tongue did not move. Augustine liked what he saw but did not hear, and he began to practise this way of reading himself.

Reading aloud nevertheless remained the culturally predominant way of absorbing the contents of a text throughout antiquity, into the Middle Ages and the new millennium, and everything that was written was first spoken aloud. Nobody had thought of writing as an independent intellectual discipline. This also suited the church and the clergy perfectly, because it gave them control over what should be written and how the written word should be read and understood. When silent reading became established in the fullness of time, the potential for rebellion against the ideas of the ruling classes opened up, whereas reading aloud, which continued to be practised in churches and meeting houses, market squares and places of entertainment, was both a way to exercise social control and a practice that bound people together. Moreover, many centuries were to pass before everyone would be granted the opportunity to learn to read.

Silent reading was first practised by the scribes in the scriptoria of monasteries, and later at the universities and among the nobility. However, this kind of reading did not become the norm until the fifteenth century; although, once it became customary, it caused a dramatic change in all kinds of intellectual work, irrespective of whether the reader was looking at handwritten manuscripts or printed pages. Silent reading was difficult unless the text had been adapted for individual use. That is why a practical punctuation system and silent reading belong together in the common, slow-moving revolution that created our civilisation.

Aristophanes constructed the first punctuation system 200 years before Christ. The subsequent development had been a rollercoaster ride, and after 1,000 years, the time was definitely ripe for a reformer with the weight of expertise behind them. The man who finally took on the task had long had good contact with fellow believers in Ireland. They shared a belief both in God and in the punctuation marks that could make it easier to read what was on his mind.

The Mini-Renaissance: For the love of God and the convenience of the reader

Alcuin and Charlemagne: The men who built Europe's written culture

Dressed in a splendid Frankish robe, King (and later Emperor) Charlemagne (AD 742–814) is seated at his table with what looks like a slate and a slate pencil. Behind him stands a man in a monk's habit. The man is Alcuin (AD 735–804), and with his right hand he guides the king's hand as he forms letters on the slate with the pencil.

Otto Rethel's vast painting of 1847 hangs at the centre of the splendid interactive museum, the Centre Charlemagne – Charles the Great's Centre – in the German city of Aachen. It was from here that Charlemagne, or 'Charles the Great', conquered and governed most of western Europe around the year 800, during the period known as the Carolingian Renaissance, which also meant good news and progress for punctuation, thanks to the emperor and our friend Alcuin.

When we hear the word Renaissance, we usually think of the period beginning in the 1400s and the renewed interest in the art and literature of Ancient Greece and Rome, and especially the ensuing cultural and economic prosperity in the heart of the land we now call Italy. *Renaissance* means rebirth, and this was already happening during the reign of

Charlemagne, when works of literature from antiquity were taken out and dusted off. Europe was given a foretaste of what was to come. Charlemagne was the king of the Franks and Lombards and eventually became Holy Roman Emperor, ruling an area that included large parts of the European mainland with Aachen (Aix-la-Chapelle) at its centre. Prior to that the cultural focal point of Europe had always been south of the Alps. Charlemagne moved it northwards, but why to Aachen in particular? More than anything, this was because of the many thermal springs in the area; he liked to swim and bathe.

Aachen today is a pleasant German provincial city. The nearest airport is Maastricht in the Netherlands, and the museum, the city's foremost attraction, has a French name. Charlemagne has been called the father of Europe, and we are right in the centre of the part of Europe to which this refers. Incidentally, he fathered quite a number of children. Among the historical findings of the British geneticist Adam Rutherford is the fact that any European who can trace his ancestry far enough back will eventually find Charlemagne. Be that as it may, in this book our attention must focus on his efforts in the field of written language.

Charlemagne could read both Greek and Latin, but he struggled with learning to write. It was not that he did not wish to do so; he simply could not manage it. This may be due to the fact that he was already an adult before he tried to learn to write. In addition, his hands were badly battered after countless wars and battles. He slept with writing materials, probably a slate and pencil, under his pillow so that he could use the late evenings to practise. He also received great help from Alcuin, but he never achieved his aim of learning to write properly. On the other hand, he was very successful in making a major investment in the teaching of writing throughout the Carolingian Empire, and the man who made Charles's dreams come true was Alcuin.

Alcuin came from York in the north of England. He was born into a noble family in AD 735 and in his youth he was educated by Egbert, who later became Archbishop of York. This made him a suitable candidate to become the head of the city's cathedral school. As the archbishop's trusted employee, in AD 781 he was honoured with the mission to travel all the way to Rome to obtain the Pope's agreement for York to continue to be an episcopal city. As chance would have it, on the way home Alcuin made a stop in the city of Parma, south of the Alps. During his stay there he met Charlemagne. They had met once before, and Alcuin liked Charles very much. In Parma the two got on so well that Alcuin was immediately invited to Aachen to teach the Emperor's children and other gifted boys. Later he was entrusted with further, more important tasks. He became head of the castle library and supreme head of the school in the Emperor's palace in Aachen, and assistant teachers came there both from Ireland and from Anglo-Saxon settlements in England.

The teaching in Aachen was inspired by the seven liberal arts of ancient Rome. *Septem artes liberales* were made up of two divisions:

- *Trivium*:
  - Logic is the art of thinking. It teaches us how to use valid arguments in order to reach sound conclusions.
  - Grammar concerns reading and writing – how to combine words correctly in sentences. And if you think grammar sounds boring, you should know that the word grammar is related to glamour, a word that originates from Scots. Both words concern magic and

       have associations with enchantment, a fine way of talk-
       ing – the power to charm.
   – Rhetoric is the art of communication or, more
       precisely, the skill that enables us to make people stop
       and listen. It also teaches us how to combine sentences
       into entire compositions that are coherent and have
       the power, clarity and beauty we strive to achieve.
- *Quadrivium*:
  - Arithmetic (the lore of numbers).
  - Geometry.
  - Music.
  - Astronomy.

In order to hone the youngsters' brains, Alcuin wrote mathe-
matical textbooks. However, he concentrated on the linguistic
disciplines from the first three liberal arts. He oversaw the
collection of copies of books from Ancient Greece and Rome
for the library in Aachen, as well as manuscripts from all over
Europe, and these formed the basis of his teaching. He established scriptoria, where diligent scribes copied these collec-
tions of ancient texts. He wrote learned books on grammar
and language, and he was among those who understood that
punctuation was valuable. Unfortunately, many people still
practised *scriptio continua* – texts without spaces between the
words and with the least possible punctuation. Alcuin himself
liked the simple system with two marks that was based on what
our Greek friend Aristophanes had thought up 1,000 years
earlier:

- *distinctio*: placed at the top of the last word to mark the
  end of a sentence.
- *subdistinctio*: placed lower down to mark a pause in the
  sentence.

In a letter to Charlemagne, Alcuin expressed his enthusiasm for this system, partly because the punctuation marks could also look like an attractive embellishment of the texts. He suggested that the skill of punctuation should be greatly improved. He feared that the lack of cultural education among the elite of the empire had weakened proficiency in punctuation. Something needed to be done to put a stop to this unfortunate development.

And he knew what to do. As a de facto minister of information for the Carolingian Empire, Alcuin's word was law. He used his influence to take an important step towards liberating the written text, making it an independent way of using the language, something that was different from and more than just a record of literary content to be read aloud. This also meant that those who inserted punctuation laid more weight than previously on how the texts were assembled grammatically in order to get the message across.

As long as scribes continued to write without spaces between the words, it was difficult in practice to insert punctuation marks. So Alcuin and his employees created a script of their own that solved the problem. *Minuscules* are small letters, which are easier to read than CAPITALS. Carolingian minuscules were well-proportioned, easy to learn to write and easy to read – and they left space for punctuation marks. Minuscules soon became popular, and Irish monks were also delighted with them. A hundred years later, they were introduced in Spain, England and Hungary.

The written language was so strong in Aachen that in 805 Charlemagne himself ordered that those employed to write should not make mistakes, and those who did not punctuate correctly should be punished. And this was all for the love of God and the convenience of the reader. In an article on book production in the Carolingian Empire, David Ganz specifies in more detail what this convenience might consist of: the quality of the text, clear script and layout and an idea of how the written language may guide the reader.

Alcuin retired in 796 at the age of 61. He spent his last eight years in the monastery of Saint Martin in the French city of Tours. But even there, he was tirelessly active. He kept the monks busy and sent some of them to York to fetch rare texts he himself had looked after as a young man far away in the north of England. York had not forgotten him, and he is still remembered there. The University of York has a college named in honour of the hero of writing: Alcuin College.

The Professor from Europe's Oldest University: Simplest is best

Boncompagno da Signa (circa AD 1170–1240) hated grammar. Could that have been the reason why he launched a super-simple form of punctuation? Chaos had reigned among the scribes of the High Medieval Period, despite Alcuin's heroic efforts. New ways of using old and new punctuation marks were continually being presented. The man who created the simplest system occupied a chair at what was then the foremost intellectual centre of Europe.

Alma mater studiorum. 'Nourishing mother of studies', no less, but it was more than vain ornamentation when the University of Bologna attached this label to itself. Until the High Middle Ages, the church had been in charge of all higher education, with the responsibility and power that followed from such a position. In 1088 bright sparks in Bologna broke this monopoly of knowledge by establishing Europe's first university. It is still possible today to sense and perceive the over 900-year-long history of the university along the pavements of Bologna's narrow streets, in the squares and inside the walls of the university buildings that are spread around in the city centre. The city is proud of its history.

Boncompagno da Signa?
The hosts who were to welcome guests at the University of Bologna did not recognise the name. They could not find anything in their computers. There was no information, no bust, no painting.

But try the archives!
We can rely on archivists. Like archivists everywhere, in Bologna they are to be found in tiny offices on the fourth floor in the middle of the narrowest corridor. But they know their way around the labyrinth and they find Boncompagno in historical documents. He is hidden in subordinate clauses inserted in papers that hardly anyone has glanced at in this millennium. Surely he deserves better? I believe we must say that these inserted subordinate clauses should be promoted to the status of independent main clauses.

Boncompagno grew up in the village of Signa just to the west of Florence, where he later went to study. As a very young man he travelled further away, to the university of Bologna, where he later became a professor, teaching rhetoric and grammar. He absolutely hated the latter discipline; it was rhetoric that really meant something to him. And here Boncompagno obviously had something to build on, as he is among those discussed in Brenda Deen Schildgen's book *The Rhetoric Canon*, in company with such notable figures as Homer, Plato, Aristotle, Socrates, Cicero, Dante, Kant and Adorno. However, it is mainly his innovative simplification of the smallest building bricks of written language that justifies his presence in this book.

Boncompagno's punctuation system made do with two marks:

- *Virgula planus:* –
  This sign marks the end of a complete idea, i.e. it plays the same role as the full stop, exclamation mark and question mark do today.
- *Virgula suspensiva:* /
  This sign marks a shorter pause, where the meaning is not yet complete.

Boncompagno did not think we needed any more punctuation marks. Nobody knows how many people used his system, but his *virgula suspensiva* was an important staging post on the way to the comma as we know it today, which was created and introduced in Venice 300 years later. That would probably have pleased the professor from Bologna, even though he was personally mainly preoccupied with rhetoric and less with grammar and formalities of that kind. Boncompagno's view was a reaction against the growing number of scholars who perceived grammar almost as a science. He wanted instead to build on oral tradition in order to produce elegant speech. He wrote a total of 17 books, most of which were about how advocates could win their point with their words or the art of letter-writing: *ars dictaminis*. His best known books are *Rhetorica Antiqua* (1215) and *Rhetorica Novissima* (1235). In them he showed nothing but disdain for Cicero, the hero of Ancient Roman rhetoric, who, in his opinion, made simple things difficult. Nor did he show any mercy towards the learned biblical scholars of the rival French university of Orléans, whom he criticised for placing far too much emphasis on formal grammar. Boncompagno believed he was promoting a modern version of Latin, whereas in France, the ideals were more complex. We can recognise the same difference in their national cuisines. Italian cooking is simple and uses few ingredients, whereas French cuisine is artfully ornamental.

Grammar and rhetoric were two of the three disciplines in the *trivium*, the first part of the medieval idea of the seven liberal arts. Boncompagno considered rhetoric to be the foremost of these subjects but he was forced to admit that grammar was an essential element of the education of beginners. He had himself undergone 16 months of grammar teaching in Florence.

Boncompagno has been described as a person with an inflated self-image. Nowadays we would have said he was arrogant or big-headed. He considered himself to be famous in Bologna, but when he tried to get a post in Rome he received nothing but rejections. His life came to a full stop – or maybe a last *virgula planus* – in a hospital in Florence, a poor and forgotten man. Or maybe not quite forgotten. It is at least possible to imagine that Boncompagno is the professor giving a lecture to the students in the reliefs and other works of art in Bologna's splendid Museo Medievale.

Outside the museum young students from all over the world are discussing medieval art. Bologna positively reeks of knowledge. Fortunately it is not all old, and maybe what the students do in the museum garden is to search for what Boncompagno considered the best inspiration for oral presentations: fresh air and sweet herbs.

The Italian Renaissance:
Our Hero from Venice

He inserted the first modern comma and the first semicolon, and he gave the world the paperback. There are many reasons to celebrate the Italian typographer, humanist, publisher, editor and translator Aldo Manuzio. He was to the culture of writing what the founder of Apple, Steve Jobs, became for the development of our everyday digital life. They were both visionaries, hard-working innovators who managed to attract able people when they wanted innovations that could replace inconvenient solutions for the few with something that worked efficiently for the many. Whereas Jobs became the symbol for innovations that made us all digital, Manuzio was the man who made written culture accessible to a broader range of social strata. And there is actually a connection between Manuzio and Jobs. 1985 saw the introduction of the Aldus PageMaker (now Adobe PM) computer program for desktop publishing, which was tailored for Apple Macintosh computers. Why Aldus? That is our man Aldo's name in Latin! (in full, Aldus Manutius).

He was active in Venice, but was born in Bassiano, a picturesque medieval town on a hill in Lazio, an hour or so by car to the south of Rome. As you drive into the town you see a fellow standing stiffly by the roadside. He is made of bronze but when the July winds from Africa bring the temperature close to 40 degrees, he looks as if he is sweating. Aldo

Manuzio surveys the traffic entering his home town, where he was born in around 1449. He is not a generally well-known historical figure, but he is a celebrity in literary circles all over the world, and Bassiano knows how to appreciate him. The town has its own Manuzio museum and invites its citizens to annual festivities in his memory.

At a very young age Aldo travelled to Rome to learn Latin. He continued his studies in Ferrara, concentrating mainly on the study of Classical Greek. Later he travelled to Capri, where Prince Lionello Pio engaged him as tutor to his sons Lionello II and Alberto. It was also here that he began to work on writing textbooks about his life's great passion – grammar.

When Aldo arrived in Venice in 1489, he was already aged 40. He had devoted his life to grammar, teaching and classical philosophy, both Greek and Latin. He came to Venice when the city was at the height of its political, economic and cultural power and, as Aldo later described it, more like a whole world than just a city. In 1492, the humanist Marsilio Ficino (1433–99) wrote that the century had been a golden age for what he called the liberal arts, which for him included poetry, painting, sculpture, architecture and song in addition to rhetoric and grammar. So we are now in the decades when Leonardo da Vinci painted his famous fresco of *The Last Supper*, Michelangelo carved his statue of David and Niccolò Machiavelli had begun to prepare the draft of *The Prince* – while Christopher Columbus and his little fleet had left Palos de la Frontera to discover new continents. And the first stones were being trundled into what we now know as St Peter's Square in Rome.

Venice was the European capital of publishers and print shops, and Manuzio became fascinated by books as the source of undreamt-of power and influence in the world. He lived in a society of economic and cultural progress, but not even Venice was protected from war and crisis. In the foreword to a book on the writings of Aristotle, Manuzio wrote that it was the destiny of the age to live in times of tragedy and turmoil, and that men turned more readily to arms than to books. He emphasised that this was the reason why he would be unable to rest until he had provided the world with a solid supply of books. And he kept his word, as 130 titles were issued by his publishing house Aldine in the period 1495 to 1515.

In 1493 Manuzio had a Latin grammar ready for printing and he thus came into direct contact with the most important players in the printing industry. His publishing house was established just over a year later near the Campo San Paolo. Here he laid the foundation stone for what was to become Europe's leading company in the field of the written word – a historic fact that the tourist magnet of Venice does its best to ignore 500 years later. Nevertheless, behind the doors of a modest establishment that produces and sells paper products, the face of the owner lit up when the name of Manuzio was mentioned. 'Go along the Calle Bernardo, cross the canal to the Calle del Scaleter. Follow the street all the way down to the Rio Terà Secondo.'

And he was right! That is where it stood, and by it is a simple plaque that modestly relates the first words of the story of Aldo Manuzio.

In a few years he built up the model company of Aldine, famous for its capacity to combine the demand for high-quality aesthetics and content with business sense and a nose for the interests and needs of a reading middle class. The goldsmith and metalworker Johannes Gutenberg had already invented the art of printing, but it was the powerful media environment of Venice that put the technological innovation to good use in order to print books for a wider reading public.

Aldo Manuzio was the first among equals in his industry, and he also drew inspiration from other fields of expertise. After a great deal of thought, the Franciscan friar Luca Pacioli (1447–1517) had worked out the principles of double entry bookkeeping, which became an essential of modern business economics. Erasmus of Rotterdam (1466–1536) is now famous as the man who gave his name to the funding programme that sends students from all over Europe on exchanges. In his own times, Erasmus was the foremost humanist on the continent and the teacher of the whole of Europe. He also spent long periods south of the Alps, but the person he most admired in Italy was not the pope – it was Aldo Manuzio! Erasmus visited Aldo in Venice, worked there and had his collection of literary proverbs *Adagia* printed by Aldine. His circle of acquaintances also included prosperous noblemen and artists, and the young painter Albrecht Dürer (1471–1528) from Nuremberg actually came to visit him during a study tour of the south.

Manuzio looked up to Germany. Book printing had been invented there, and the country also represented the political reforms he had a liking for. On the other hand, many fledgling German printers had emigrated to Italy, where literary life was more vigorous than in their homeland. So Manuzio remained in Venice. The city offered him inspiration of many kinds. As a publisher, Aldo the grammarian soon developed an overall view of text production that also included design, illustrations and the physical qualities of the book – its size and paper quality – and always kept the public's visual needs in mind.

He had a lot to offer, and we should not be surprised if it was over a substantial carafe of red wine from Trentino that he confessed late one evening:

Ma ho una piccola idea anch'io. Da tempo provo e riprovo minuscoli segni da mettere tra le parole: il punto, la virgola, l'apostrofo ...

But I also have a little idea. I have been trying for a long time to put little markers between the words: the full stop, the comma, the apostrophe ... (Pacilli, 2009)

It was not a little idea, it was a great one, and in reality Manuzio was grappling with not just one but many ideas:

- In 1495 he established how the comma and semicolon should be set in type, and he also worked out grammar-based rules for modern punctuation. Better communication!
- He developed the *italic* (cursive) style of writing and the *roman* font that is still used every day in the form of Times New Roman. Both of these innovations were inspired by inscriptions from Roman times and decorations from the architecture of antiquity – aesthetics played a central role in Manuzio's many interests. To give the letters perfect proportions he had help from the friar, economist and mathematician Luca Pacioli.
- He had printing ink made that could stand sunlight – and it was used on the finest paper available at the time.
- Manuzio reissued the works of antiquity in a form that was accessible to a wider public, either in the original Latin or Greek or translated into Italian. He also presented new literature.
- In 1501 the house published works by the Roman poet Virgil (70–19 BC) in a miniature format, and the following year, the works of Italy's national poet Dante Alighieri (1265–1321) were published in the same pocket format. The paperback had been invented!

This format rapidly became popular with travelling merchants, diplomats, military officers and others who needed books in a handy format for their leisure time. Now they could read while waiting between two meetings or on their journey by horse caravan between assignments in different places.

• Manuzio's books were also innovative through the introduction of text in two columns, lists of contents and pagination. The innovations represented by Manuzio also produced profitable results. His edition of Petrarch's *Canzoniere* was printed and sold in an edition of 100,000 copies.

We do not know exactly when Aldo Manuzio was born, but we know that he died in 1515. His death occurred on 16th April of that year, and the date has since become World Semicolon Day. Put a cross on your calendar! We also know that Manuzio created the modern book; he is the one we have to thank when we take a paperback with us to read in the bath, in bed or in a café. In many ways Manuzio can be seen as Europe's first editor. He combined the classical ideals with the demands encountered by a modern publisher in a democratic market economy. Manuzio was soundly educated in the humanist disciplines and wanted to promote cultural and intellectual aims, rather than simply economic goals. He published both fiction and non-fiction, he saw the value of grammatical knowledge and he was aware of the importance of design and the skills of the artisan. And he was always on the hunt for better solutions. In a de luxe volume published in connection with an exhibition in Venice in 2016 on Aldo Manuzio and the Renaissance, the editors, Guido Beltramini and Davide Gasparotto, summarised the essence of Manuzio's work as an editor in the following words:

Aldo was an awesome editor. His concern for the text was meticulous and uncompromising, and the leading philologists of the past were involved. The secret weapons of Aldo's books were content, structure, clarity and harmony.

Today's editors in the media and in publishing houses can also find inspiration in all those things. And we can all be inspired by the motto of Aldo Manuzio's publishing house: *Festina lente* (make haste slowly). The motif for the logo was an anchor and dolphin, the anchor representing stability and the dolphin energy and speed. The motto and logo became an expression of lasting worth, and Herman Melville even wrote in one of his versions of *Moby-Dick* about the printer, the dolphin and the anchor, though he transformed the dolphin into a whale.

Gutenberg invented the art of printing, but Manuzio made use of the technology and developed it further. Gutenberg's invention can be compared to the first computers: they were important but also very large, clumsy and not very practical. Just as innovators like Steve Jobs transformed mammoths into everyday tools for you and me, Manuzio perfected the invention of printing with his many innovations and improvements in the field.

What Aldo Manuzio did in 1494 was not only to invent new ways of depicting punctuation marks; he also set in motion the standardisation of a punctuation system that helped to make the written language a supreme means of communication, 1,700 years after the Greek chief librarian Aristophanes had constructed the first simple system of punctuation.

Es ist vollbracht (It is finished), it says in John 19:30 in the Bible printed by Johannes Gutenberg in 1455 – the time of birth of the art of printing in the western world. The printing press was one of civilisation's most important innovations; it created the hardware for the new art. It was absolutely essential, but in order to be effective and practical it needed the equivalent software. When Gutenberg had done the spadework, further development was taken over by printing houses throughout large parts of central Europe, and in particular in the two Italian cities of Venice and Florence, which were the Silicon Valley of their day. They attracted creative, thoughtful and questioning people from all over Europe, and they could also provide the capital to finance the multitude of new ideas. This resulted in innovations in most fields of science, art, industry and commerce.

Production methods for the printed word were also further developed and perfected, and our man, Aldo Manuzio, was at the centre, as both an innovator and a driving force. He was not only a printer but also a humanist, editor and publisher, and he created completely new forms of arranging text, including particularly a system of punctuation that we have retained for over 500 years. So it is appropriate to say that it was finished – or rather perfected – in 1494.

As for the comma and the semicolon, they were invented once and for all.

When the time came, the publishing house was taken over first by the family of Aldo's father-in-law, then by Aldo's son Paolo and later by his grandson Aldo the Younger, who continued the family's proud traditions, although he was the last member of the publishing dynasty. The publishing house was closed shortly after his death in 1597, after more than 100 years of epoch-making cultural work.

In 1566, Aldo the Younger published *Orthographiae ratio*, an account of all the marks and rules of modern punctuation. Here for the first time it was stated clearly in one place that the purpose of commas, full stops, colons and semicolons is to clarify the syntax – the way sentences are constructed. Previously punctuation marks had mainly been used to make it easier to read the text aloud. Now grammatical considerations were elevated and given the central position.

The Manuzio family established the visual appearance of punctuation marks and how they should be used. The age of printing coincided with the spread of the humanist ideas that arose in the Renaissance, first of all in Italy, and with the Manuzios as their dedicated and efficient promulgators. The principles of punctuation adopted by the humanists were used in the production and distribution of copies of texts from antiquity and of course when the new texts of the Renaissance were to be presented and published in book form. Later they left their mark on punctuation in all western European languages, though with variations in the extent to which they included considerations of rhythm and pauses – rhetorical punctuation. Rules and practice vary only slightly from language to language. Manuzio's principles have also influenced the punctuation of languages such as Russian, Sanskrit, Arabic, Hebrew, Chinese and Japanese.

Epilogue

Technology contributed to the standardisation of punctuation as well as to a leap forward in many other areas, such as industrialisation and economic growth, nation-building, language development and democratisation. In addition, the spread of books and writings using standardised punctuation and typography led to greater individualisation, because every reader could now develop his own individual thought world. The ideas that were disseminated led to a further increase in knowledge, but that was not the end of it; the new mass distribution of information prepared the ground for new ideas and human growth in all areas of life.

Everyone – within the limits set by economic resources and reading skills – could sit in his closet imbibing texts old and new and interpret the content freely and independently, without the interference of rulers and finger-wagging authorities – whether spiritual or secular. The social networks surrounding the written word also changed. The authoritarian culture of the era of oral communication and the production of isolated copies of books disappeared in a transformation that, in the fullness of time, generated and shaped a middle-class public. The space for free, unbounded utterances expanded dramatically, although this did not always please the powers that be. The reaction came in the form of harsh censorship. The right to free speech had to fight hard against repression and subjugation in the sixteenth and seventeenth centuries.

In the 1960s, the Canadian media theorist and historian Marshall McLuhan described the transition from the written to the printed word as the gateway to a Gutenberg era that has lasted until our time and is still in existence in many ways, though it is now under pressure from digital technology. McLuhan believed that the book did for the eye what the wheel did for the feet. One of his memorable sayings was that the medium is the message. The social consequences of changes in the system of transporting information are greater than the consequences of changes to the message itself. In McLuhan's view, the creation of a common punctuation system was more significant than what was written. Most of us would consider that this view would be stretching things too far; it is impossible to ignore the explosive potential of what can be conveyed by the printed word. The church reformer Martin Luther (1483–1546) was one of those who knew how to exploit the new technology. Together with the market economy, the Protestant ethic he represented was a driving force in the development of western and northern Europe.

Punctuation marks are powerful in many ways. This book is about punctuation, but that is an imprecise description, as it deals specifically with the punctuation marks used in the culture of western writing. There are other systems of punctuation in other parts of the world. Some are similar to our system and some are different. In a book on punctuation, art and politics, the American writer Jennifer DeVere Brody argues in favour of the idea that those who have the strongest military forces determine how the language is to be written. She writes about a western idea of our phonetic alphabet as the superior one and punctuation as a western export to many Asian countries under the heading of post-colonisation, and makes a connection between ink and blood.

Aldus Manutius inserted the first comma in print in 1494, two years after his Italian compatriot Christopher Columbus had discovered America. These two events can be said to represent the great step being taken by Europe. Ways of thinking, living and production were changing and Europe was moving into the global driving seat. What was happening to China? For several thousand years the Chinese had been technologically superior to the Europeans. Paper came into use 1,000 years earlier than in Europe and books were printed as early as the seventh century. At the very time when Europe was gathering speed, China was stagnating. There may have been several reasons. The Spanish sociologist Manuel Castells points to the role of the Chinese state. For a long time, the state apparatus had stimulated development, but from the fifteenth century on, a desire to hold on to power and maintain the status quo led to stagnation, both in the state itself and among the social elite who wanted to be on good terms with the country's leadership. The driving forces for change disappeared and at the same time China became isolated from ideas in the wider world and entered a period of stagnation that lasted for several hundred years. In the meantime Europe was undergoing an enormous economic, technological, social and cultural metamorphosis.

On a smaller scale, at the end of the last millennium, the French sociologist Pierre Bourdieu became a star of popular culture through his research based on such concepts as economic, social and cultural capital. He wrote that tastes and understanding of reality are different in each social class and that these differences cement and reflect control. In our context it is indisputable that the mastery of punctuation is a kind of cultural capital that can be converted into social small change: the comma of rulers is the ruling comma, and a linguistic situation is never purely a matter of linguistics.

Bourdieu wrote of the Paris riots in 1968 that the trendsetting classes were willing to die for French orthography. And there are also mastery techniques for demonstrating that learning the rules for commas is not sufficient in order to be accepted into the upper classes. Bourdieu cited the then French president Valéry Giscard d'Estaing as an example. He definitely belonged in the top level of the French elite, but occasionally chose to make careless mistakes with verb endings in order to distance himself from lower-middle-class hyper-correctness. A strategic indifference specifically in relation to comma rules is mentioned by Bourdieu in his major work *Distinction*, from 1979. When intellectuals deliberately break the rules, it is a strategy for preventing access to the elite by those who believe one can become intellectual solely by following the rules.

Punctuation is one of the most splendid things our civilisation has produced, in a glorious development leading from antiquity via the Renaissance and through to our times. The opportunities to succeed with what we write are better for those who master the comma rules than for those who do not wish to learn or use them. The author Lynne Truss is Britain's best-known champion of correct punctuation. Her response to claims that rules of punctuation are a way of oppressing the uneducated is: *Pah!* Truss writes that punctuation is no more a class issue than the air we breathe, and she has recorded the fact that the ability and will to punctuate correctly is evenly divided across the classes. Her suggestion is that, instead of criticising punctuation, we should passionately celebrate what it has contributed to our culture for half a millennium.

So it may well be as Bourdieu maintains, that putting commas in the right place does not necessarily give you a place in the most sophisticated salons.

By the beginning of the seventeenth century, punctuation marks had become fixed. What occurred later were adjustments and changes of taste and preference, and also a spread of punctuation to new areas of language. For a long time, English was an insignificant West Germanic language, with elements of Old Norse and Celtic, and a considerable proportion of words of French origin. But in line with Britain's political and economic expansion and her position at the centre of a vast colonial empire, over the years English became the fashionable language of the west.

The actor, poet and playwright Ben Jonson was the first to take punctuation seriously during the English Renaissance. He saw the importance of small details. So he changed his original surname, Johnson, to Jonson and put a colon between his forename and surname as archbishops and professors did. In his *English Grammar*, written in 1617 and published in 1640, he wrote about an English punctuation system inspired by the humanists on the continent. They considered the text to be an organic whole, in which attention must be paid to the presence of the author. Logical grammatical analysis was Jonson's starting point for the idea that this kind of analysis can form the basis for clarifying the individual elements of the text. However, Jonson did not ignore the rhetorical function of punctuation for indicating the oral delivery of the text. And lastly, the humanists – and Ben Jonson – were preoccupied with the possibilities that punctuation marks offered for making the nuances of the text easy to understand.

In practice, the result of taking all these considerations into account was a heavy, dense punctuation that we would nowadays call *overpunctuation*, as in these lines from Jonson's play *The Alchemist* (Act II, Scene 3):

If you, my Sonne, should, now, preuaricate,
And, to your owne particular lusts, employ
So great, and catholique a blisse; Be sure,
A curse will follow, yea, and ouertake
Your subtle, and most secret ways.

In the years that followed, punctuation was overemphasised. If there was a phrase or a sentence where a comma could be placed both before and after it, the opportunity was eagerly seized. Throughout the eighteenth and nineteenth centuries, only this heavy punctuation was accepted. A lighter form of punctuation was not approved and implemented until the early 1900s in English and speech communities influenced by English. For its part, the German speech community retained a grammar-based punctuation system, which was also adopted by the Danes. Norway held on to Danish punctuation for a long time, and there were many rules. As recently as 1900, Norwegian pupils in elementary schools had to struggle through 34 pages of comma rules in the book *Kommaregler: Udgave for børn* (Comma Rules: Children's Edition). Seven years later the rules were changed. The principle of rhetorical punctuation was established, even though grammar-based rules were continued. Over the years, the result was nevertheless a freer and lighter form of punctuation in Norway, as in most other countries.

And then the internet arrived. More on this in Part 3, 'A Philosophy for a World in Motion'.

PART II

Civilising Marks

Correct usage is a premise for moral clarity and honesty. Many a dirty trick and violent abuse of power arise when grammar and syntax are messed up. (. . .) This indeed is why a single misplaced comma can result in disasters, can cause fires that destroy the woods on this Earth.

Claudio Magris, Italian professor of German

The American author Ernest Hemingway (1899–1961) often used to lunch with fellow authors at the Algonquin Hotel in New York. During one of these lunches – so the story goes – the authors were discussing how short a story can be. Six words are enough, was Hemingway's opinion. 'OK, if you can do that, we'll each give you ten dollars,' replied his companions. Hemingway thought for a bit, then he wrote on a napkin:

Baby shoes: for sale. Never worn.

Hemingway won the bet.

You come home one evening. You are met by a six-word story. On the chest of drawers under the mirror in the hall there is a note for you:

The time is ripe for something new.

How do you interpret this message? And how would punctuation marks other than the full stop have changed your interpretation? There are numerous possibilities:

The time is ripe for something new.
The time is ripe for something new!
The time is ripe for something new?
The time is ripe for something new ...

The time is ripe for something new –
The time is ripe for something new
The time is ripe for something new!?
The time is ripe for something new!!!

If the person writing is addicted to emojis, you might also have been met like this:

The time is ripe for something new :)
The time is ripe for something new ;)
The time is ripe for something new :(

All the same, we get a long way with the classic punctuation marks. They are still most important when we write, especially in formal and/or professional contexts. And, as the example shows, they do more than separate or link sentences or parts of sentences. They can also express feelings, emphasise the words or moderate them.

Which punctuation mark would you most like to be met by on a note on the chest in the hall?

Punctuation is a system, as well as being a part of the great system of writing:

• Macro level: How should you organise the text? What arguments and factors should you use?
• Meso level: How do you create clear, effective sentences and paragraphs?
• Micro level: How can grammar contribute to logic when you write? What is the best way to use punctuation marks for good communication? How are words spelt?

Punctuation also has several levels. Punctuation has a visual aspect if we wear glasses to magnify text on a page or see it at a distance. The Greeks began dividing text into paragraphs with extra space between the lines. Throughout antiquity and on into the Middle Ages, many learned scribes attempted to insert spaces between the words. Our friend Aldo Manuzio placed great emphasis on grammar and punctuation, but he also saw the value of making the layout of the text look attractive and accessible. Nothing, empty space, what printers and typographers call white space, is also a sign to the reader about how the text should be understood. Paragraphs were introduced early on in the development of writing. Later on the text was indented to indicate a substantial pause, and capital letters came into use. Spacing between words gradually became established practice. This purely visual aspect does not feature in the book you are now reading.

At the micro level of punctuation, we find marks that are important, for example for pronunciation. In this large group we find things like accents, apostrophes, hyphens, hashtags and quotation marks. These marks also fall outside the scope of this book.

Our attention here will focus on punctuation marks. Some of them are very important, others are merely important. The full stop is definitely the most important. Grammarians stress the fact that the main role of the full stop is to set boundaries between complete sentences. Those who are preoccupied by the idea that punctuation marks should reflect the spoken word would say that the full stop marks a longer pause than other marks. The Swedish writer Vilhelm Moberg described it thus in 1935:

There are three punctuation marks in the world: the little one, the half-big and the big one. They are called comma, semicolon and full stop. At a comma you should pause a little, just a little – just as long as it takes to blink once. At a semicolon you should stop twice as long – or two blinks. But at a full stop you should pause and give yourself plenty of time while you exhale a whole breath.

The Swedish writer and translator Alva Dahl has written a treatise on the use of punctuation in three Swedish novels. Here is her introduction to the term *interpunktion-stextur* (punctuation patterns), which gives a visual representation of how punctuation can vary. She uses two variables:

- Is the punctuation dense or sparse? Dense punctuation means that the author uses many punctuation marks; sparse means that punctuation marks are rare.
- Is the punctuation heavy or light? Apart from division into paragraphs and indentation, the full stop is the heaviest mark, followed by the semicolon, colon, dash and comma. Dahl considers the division into heavy and light marks as analogous to the listing of punctuation marks in earlier times in a hierarchical order according to the length of the pause, as in the quotation from Vilhelm Moberg above.

Alva Dahl regards the punctuation pattern as a rhythmical structure, in which the heavier and denser parts often actualise the formal content. Parts of the text with lighter, sparser punctuation may indicate simultaneity of content or fast tempo. Her conclusion is that the choice of punctuation marks has great importance for which information is highlighted in the foreground and which is treated as background information.

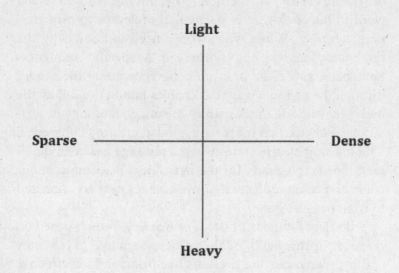

As writers, we use punctuation marks in different ways, and we do not use them in the same way from one text to another. How do you punctuate when you are writing a job application? Or when you send a text to your partner? The diagram comes from Alva Dahl.

Many traditional aspects of research have something to contribute when it comes to punctuation. This has traditionally been the province of philologists, but in recent years there has also been research into how the brain registers and processes texts. The American psychologist Steven Pinker is engaged in this research. In his book *The Sense of Style*, he praises grammar. He describes it as our very first division app(lication). Grammar tells us how the building bricks of language should be combined. In Pinker's opinion, when we have mastered grammar, we will be capable of writing clearly, correctly and beautifully. And there is a word in his book that is particularly relevant to punctuation: *coherence*. When we read, we need to know why the sentences follow one another in a specific sequence. Sentences with clear internal coherence guide the reader through the text in a way that enables him/her to follow the message, without timewasting, misunderstandings or irritations. Punctuation marks are good at creating coherence. The full stop clearly states when a message has been delivered. The text is ready for the next one. The comma, semicolon and colon indicate that what comes next is connected to what has just gone.

Yellowlees Douglas's book *The Reader's Brain* is based on research in the fields of linguistics, cognitive psychology and neuroscience. She presents five principles for effective writing. They all begin with C in English, and three of them are *coherence*, *continuity* and *cadence*. We recognise coherence as the internal coherence of the (thought in the) text. Continuity covers flow and forward thrust. According to Douglas, the answer here lies between the sentences. How the sentences are divided and linked together is very important for understanding. Once again punctuation makes a contribution. Douglas's third principle, cadence, is to do with rhythm, for example the variation between long and short sentences. Punctuation also delivers in this case. Short sentences divided by full stops create a rhythm that can be both brief and staccato. Longer sentences with a large number of commas can produce both speed and calm, depending on whether the alternative is full stops or no punctuation.

Punctuation really has a lot to offer. It is not possible for a person who can write to live without putting in full stops. We also use exclamation marks and question marks to set grammatical borderlines, and they indicate pauses of about the same length as a full stop. They are also handy when we want to ask about something or express a feeling or an intention.

The comma is a useful aid when we write, but that is not the reason it belongs in a class by itself. The reason for all the attention paid to commas is the uncertainty about how they should be used. This uncertainty drives schoolchildren to despair, creates doubt and belief and is the source of quarrels and disputes. Was there a comma missing there? I could have written: *This uncertainty drives schoolchildren to despair, creates doubt and belief, and is the source of quarrels and disputes.* The comma is the punctuation mark where we can most clearly see the meeting point between grammatical and rhetorical thinking (the idea that we should punctuate to make it easy to read aloud). Sometimes these principles conflict, and what do we do then? It is not by chance that the chapter on the comma takes up the largest number of pages in the remainder of the book.

Then we have a few other punctuation marks. Colons are useful but unproblematic. Parentheses, dashes and ellipses (. . .) also belong here and can be used in small doses. Then we have the semicolon. That may be called an optional mark, and you can manage very well without it. But why should you reject the offer? Everyone should treat themselves to an occasional semicolon!

Punctuation marks emphasise the logic of what you write. They support your internal and external voice with indications of rhythm and intonation. But the most important thing of all is their capacity to make the reader understand quickly and efficiently what you want to achieve when you write.

They indicate the boundaries of items of information and the connections between the items; they indicate the sense and feelings in what you write and choreograph and orchestrate your thoughts.

He came to the river.
The river was there.
Ernest Hemingway

When the Final Word Has Been Written

For 2,200 years the full stop has been a simple, stable, unobtrusive partner for people who write. It has not made much of an impression, apart from fulfilling its only task: to inform readers that the message has been delivered. But things are now beginning to happen to the full stop. In rapid digital messages we no longer see it as unfeeling, so we now use it in a different way from previously.

If you google 'comma mistake', you get 18 million hits. If you google 'full stop mistake' instead, it goes down to a miserable 500,000 hits – and many of those are about mistakes in the use of commas. The silence surrounding the full stop is in inverse proportion to its importance, as the full stop is quite simply indispensable. If need be, we can get by without the other punctuation marks for a long time, but it is impossible to write without putting in an occasional full stop. That is how it occurred in antiquity. The Ancient Greeks realised that it might be a good idea to have a mark indicating that what has been said is said and done. Breathe out. Draw breath. Take a real break. Work out what you are going to say next. Start again. Then write down the next thing that is in your mind. Put in full stops more often. Then what we write will be less of a mess. We avoid nagging doubts about the use of commas.

Chief librarian Aristophanes inserted the first full stop when he drew up his *distinctiones* around 200 BC. He put a dot at the top when a complete thought was finished. This was the introduction of the most important of all punctuation marks and it never disappeared again. In the ninth century, the full stop moved down to the position where we find it today.

The full stop is easy to understand. We put it in when we need to delimit the statement we are uttering. We give the reader a clear message that we have delivered a complete item of information. The next sentence will contain new information. When you were at school you might have learned that sentences must have a subject and a predicate (or at least a verb). This is no longer true. We now also accept sentences that were previously considered incomplete. Like this one.

Even though a full stop is easy and unproblematic to use, it can also be used to achieve special effects. The Norwegian Armed Forces have a motto in which the full stop is used in just such an untraditional way: *For alt vi har. Og alt vi er.* (For all that we have. And all that we are.)

The full stop can also be used in commands: *Read the following pages.* Did you understand that as an impassioned order? If I wanted to add enthusiasm or power to the order, I would write: *Read the following pages!*

The full stop is easy to get along with, but occasionally it causes confusion:

- Indirect questions are not followed by a question mark but by a full stop:
  He asked what the story was about.
- If the sentence ends with an exclamation mark or a question mark, you must leave out the full stop:
  I have not read 'Who's Afraid of Virginia Wolf?'
- It the sentence ends with an abbreviation, the full stop after the abbreviation also serves as a full stop for the sentence:
  We will work with transport plans etc.

- When the sentence ends with a parenthesis, the full stop is placed outside the closing bracket:
  I walked home (because my car was broken).
- When an entire sentence is in parentheses, the full stop is placed inside the closing bracket:
  (My life had been a never-ending love story.)
- Some abbreviations end with a full stop: *Jr., a.m.*
- An ellipsis (. . .) is a sign that something has been omitted and, when used in moderation, it can effectively express hesitation or doubt or give the reader a reason for further thought.
  My life had been a never-ending story, but it was not a love story . . .

We could have stopped here, but in recent years the full stop has started to behave differently. Or is it perhaps rather that people who write see the full stop in a different way from previously? The starting point was the fact that the full stop lacks colour and volume; it adds no information to the sentence apart from the fact that the message has been delivered. If we wanted to express determination, passion or strong feelings, we used to replace the full stop with an exclamation mark! Now technology has given us opportunities to write via new channels. According to the website Data Never Sleeps, in 2017 the world population sent over 15 million text messages every single minute. The figure for the whole year is so high that I am unable to write, read or comprehend it. And in addition to these 15 million messages per minute, there is everything we write via apps like Messenger and WhatsApp.

Text-speak is the name we give to the special way we write when we communicate via messages, often in a communication that goes on in real time, with several messages going to and fro: We *chat*. Technically, we are writing, but at the same time the communication resembles a face-to-face conversation. What we lack in this chat-writing is the opportunity to modulate the message with our voice and body language. That is why we use and understand the full stop in a different way – as well as abbreviating words.

Let us say that you have received a text from a friend:

I've got a new dog. Do you want to look at it?

You can choose between two answers:

Maybe.
Maybe

How will your friend interpret the two alternatives? Three psychologists at Binghamton University in the USA have carried out a study to find the answer, and they confirmed what you would have guessed: *Maybe.* with a full stop is perceived more negatively than *Maybe* without a full stop. Similarly they found that:

- *Yes* without a full stop is perceived more positively than *Yes.* with a full stop.
- *No.* with a full stop is understood more negatively than *No* without a full stop.

When we write ordinary text in formal contexts, we insert full stops from a grammatical perspective. The sentence is complete. In addition, we like to make a longer pause after a full stop than after a semicolon or a comma. The researchers at Binghamton University found that the full stop carries out additional rhetorical tasks when we communicate informally using digital media. This means that in contexts of this kind, the full stop is no longer a neutral marker that can perform a grammatical function but now, on the contrary, conveys a message of its own. Particularly when communicating in informal situations and with people we know, we easily abandon the traditional use of the full stop. *OMG*

Has the formerly so peaceful full stop simply become aggressive? That is the opinion of a columnist in *New Republic* magazine. He believes that a full stop at the end of a sentence gives the signal: in the sentence I've just finished writing I'm a bit dissatisfied (or cross). So he has stopped putting full stops, for example in text messages:

> *Instead he starts the next sentence on a new line*
> *Many of us do the same*
> *He has noted that*
> *The question is whether the rest of us have observed the same thing*
> *And if so*
> *Have we also changed the way we use the full stop?*

Maybe the answer will depend on age and gender. When I asked adults in my social circle, I got answers like these:

> *My punctuation is still undergoing renovation*
> *I stopped using full stops when one boy pointed out that people don't use full stops on Instagram*

But when we write in formal situations at work or at school, what was imprinted on us when we learned to write still applies. More on that later.

Cut out all these exclamation points.
An exclamation point is like laughing at your own joke.
F. Scott Fitzgerald

Go on! Go on!! Go on!!!

Jacopo Alpoleio (?–1430) called this mark *punctus admirativus*. The mark of admiration! Alpoleio lived in the town of Urbisaglia in Marche near the east coast of Italy. He wrote poetry, and he thought that full stops or question marks were not sufficient when the poems were to be read aloud. How could he make it clear that the completed sentence contained an emotion? So he inserted a slightly inclined stroke, almost a comma, above the full stop. That is how the exclamation mark entered the language. It is still there in abundance, and Alpoleio has earned a permanent place in the history of language. Maybe he would have preferred to be remembered for his poetry, but he cannot be disappointed by having the honour of being credited with having enriched the written language with an innovation that has held the field for over 600 years. At all events, his native town of Urbisaglia is enthusiastic, as he is celebrated there every year with festivities and an art festival. And he must be pleased that he is considered to be the inventor of this punctuation mark, because there is also another story about the birth of the exclamation mark in circulation. *Io* in Latin means *hurrah* or *joy,* and it is written with a capital I above an O, so it also looks like an exclamation mark . . .

However, in this book we will support the poet from Urbisaglia. He must have given a lot of thought to punctuation, as he also introduced a completely different system based on the length of the pauses that fitted in with the text. Jacopo Alpoleio's system contained many new punctuation marks. He taught the system to others but it never really caught on, so we will allow it to remain forgotten – and prefer to remember him as the father of the exclamation mark, because the exclamation mark was well received as an indicator that could add colour, music and passion to the text.

The humanist Coluccio Salutati was among the first to start using the exclamation mark in the manuscripts he edited. He saw how it could make reading the text aloud clearer. When Aldo Manuzio published a grammar book in Venice in 1508, he wrote that this punctuation mark could add indignation, compassion, surprise and admiration to the text.

So it began as an expression of admiration: *punctus admirativus*. The name was soon changed to signal an extended use: *punctus exclamativus, exclamation mark*. That is what we still call it, but it has had many names. The Swedes call it a mark of desire, greeting, surprise or passion, while British names include *screamer, astonisher, bang* and *wow*.

This multitude of terms reflects the variety of ways the exclamation mark is used; it expresses emotions, and does so with a vengeance. At the same time the exclamation mark shows that the sentence is finished and the meaning is complete.

Come here!
How sad!
That's quite some dress!

Can it also be used after greetings in letters and emails? It is quite often used like this:

Hi, Kari!

Some of us write like that, at any rate if we want to express a little pleasure at greeting the recipient. It is also possible to write:

Hi, Kari
Hi, Kari.

That would be a sober, unemotional greeting. In our digital age the use of exclamation marks and emojis is increasing rapidly. If you are content with a matter-of-fact full stop at the end, you risk the recipient thinking you are cross. We do not know whether we are taking this interpretation with us when we move over into matter-of-fact, professional communication, but if you do have a feeling for it, you can follow your salutation with an exclamation mark! In English this third variant is the only possibility in formal salutations:

Dear Kari,

The exclamation mark works! All the same, the fact is that no punctuation mark apart from the semicolon is as derided and insulted as the exclamation mark. Or to be more precise: when you read advice on writing, the general theme is that exclamation marks should be used with caution. When Mark Twain was giving advice to comic strip writers in 1897, he warned them against shouting at readers with *whooping exclamation points*. The Norwegian author Erlend Loe has an even stricter approach in his book *Volvo Lastvagnar* (*Volvo trucks*):

Some may think that there should have been an exclamation mark after the previous sentence, but I (who am writing this) feel that using an exclamation mark is a sign of weakness. Maybe one can use exclamation marks twice in one's life if one writes every day. If one writes less than every day, one can in certain circumstances use an exclamation mark once. People who use exclamation marks uncritically should be interned and sent away – at least for a while.

Loe's fellow author Lars Ramslie agrees with him. In an interview with the newspaper *Morgenbladet,* Ramslie stated that linguistically speaking he had tried to restrict everything and that he used only full stops and commas in his books. 'For the last twenty years there has been an incredible number of colons, semicolons, parentheses, exclamation marks and capital letters in Norwegian literature,' he said. However, punctuation that acts out the writer's feelings was around much earlier. In his 1970 book *Arild Asnes,* the author Dag Solstad joined the fray with quadruple exclamation marks:

> *[. . .] and Arild Asnes is sickened, he had a thorough knowledge of these things, so he did not want to forgo writing a good novel about this rather than writing a dreadfully pretentious working-class novel (My goodness! Arild Asnes writes a novel with a working-class setting!!!!)*

How often should we use exclamation marks? Some advisers put a figure on the answer with a double underlining: maximum once per 500 words! Never more than one per email! Never in an academic article! The advice is well meant, but a better guideline would be to adapt the use of exclamation marks to the genre, context and purpose of the text. A sober factual report to the boss would rarely be improved by (many) exclamation marks. A love letter to him on the other hand, might easily be construed as having a double meaning if you only used full stops. But this is also a matter of your temperament. The composer Richard Wagner put it this way: *I write music with an exclamation mark!*

The Greek storyteller Aesop (620–560 BC) gives us a hint about how to reach a conclusion in the fable about the boy who was tending sheep near a village. The boy shouted 'The wolf is coming! The wolf is coming!', and people came to help him, but there was no wolf. The boy repeated this trick many times, but there was never any wolf to be seen. Eventually a wolf did come sneaking by. The boy became frightened and called for help: 'Wolf! Wolf!' But this time nobody came to help him. He had previously cried *wolf!* for no reason, so why should people believe him this time? What we writers can learn from Aesop is that the exclamation mark must be used with care and never at the wrong time. If we use it when we really mean it, it will be effective. If we misuse it, it loses its power. The American author Henry Miller (1891–1980) wrote surrealistically, often about people who lived liberated lives, but he was very strict on one point: *Keep your exclamation points under control!*

Another important rule is to make do with a single exclamation mark: *The film was so good!*

That is enough! More exclamation marks are just noise:

The film was so good!!!

And you should only enable Caps Lock if you want to appear manic or hysterical:

THE FILM WAS SO GOOD!!!!

Alcuin and his troops in Aachen invented small letters – minuscules – 1,200 years ago. They discovered that this made the text easier to read. This insight is still valid.

Then it may happen that, on a rare occasion, you want to write in a crescendo. Then do so!

Stop! Stop!! Stop!!!

One European written language uses the exclamation mark in a way that differs from the usual: Spanish. The Spanish are not content with writing an exclamation mark at the end of a sentence. In order to stress the fact that something eyebrow-raising is on the way, writers of Spanish also start the sentence with an exclamation mark, albeit one turned upside down: *¡Qué día más bonito!* (What a lovely day!) That's their business.

'Research' shows that women write more exclamation marks than men. In these studies the difference is usually interpreted as being due to the 'fact' that women misuse the exclamation mark as a result of emotional instability. The American researcher Carol Waseleski decided to look behind the figures. She analysed how 200 exclamation marks were used in two internet discussion groups. This is what she found:

- One in three exclamation marks is categorised as friendly, for example in opening or closing posts. *Hi! Good luck!*
- Another third of the exclamation marks are placed after assertions of fact: *The Earth is flat!*
- Only one exclamation mark in ten falls into the category of emotionally unacceptable; exclamation marks used aggressively, rudely, sarcastically or to be effusively grateful: *I told you: Not in the library! As if!*
- There is nothing to indicate that women use exclamation marks because they are emotionally on the brink. On the contrary, there is a slight tendency for men to use them more often in this way.

Carol Waseleski believes that the results mean that the exclamation mark is seldom used in an emotionally unstable way, but is more often used principally to indicate friendliness. If women use it more often than men, it is because women's communication (at any rate on the internet) typically expresses gratitude, recognition and a desire for fellowship through posts that are intended to make their readers feel accepted and welcome. What about men? They use fewer exclamation marks, but when they do, they also use them mainly after assertions about facts or to express friendship in a suitable way. Carol Waseleski's conclusion is that persons of both genders can convey friendship by a use of exclamation marks that is not excessive.

Another study from the United States confirms that exclamation marks are used more often to express positive than negative feelings. The researchers Hancock, Landrigan and Silver had 80 students communicate in pairs via an internet messaging service. The students were unknown to one another and were seated in separate rooms. Half the participants were asked to appear positive and the other half negative, but without saying why they were in a good or bad mood. The subsequent analysis showed that those who wished to appear positive used more words, were more in agreement with their opposite number and used more exclamation marks. In fact, the participants who were in a good mood used six times as many exclamation marks as those who were in a bad mood. And the exclamation marks were noticed: The participants who were asked to assess the mood of their opposite number understood a large number of exclamation marks as a sign that their partner was in a positive emotional state. The researchers found these results particularly interesting, because the punctuation filled the role usually played by body language, facial expression, tone and volume of voice when we communicate verbally in the same room.

So what about emojis? When the research was carried out in 2007 they were not being used to any great extent. Nowadays there would be more. Incidentally, we can note that the use of emojis did not appear to have much bearing on the extent to which the happy or sad partner was understood to be so.

The philosopher and sociologist Theodor Adorno wrote in 1956 that he saw red when he discovered an exclamation mark, but do we really pay attention to them? That is what a group of Dutch researchers wanted to find out in a social psychology experiment, in which 124 students had to assess various situations presented on a computer screen. Half the students saw an exclamation mark on the screen for one minute before they were presented with situations they had to decide about. The other half went straight to the questions they had to answer. How did it go? The group that was exposed to an exclamation mark reacted more quickly and better than the group that went straight to the issue. So the exclamation served the purpose of *Alarm!*

When Jacopo Alpoleio inserted the first exclamation mark around the year 1400, he took our civilisation a tiny bit further forward. When we talk, the words can be helped to express emotions by the way we use and modulate our voices, the expressions on our faces and the attitude of our bodies. We appear almost like living exclamation marks. Alpoleio wrote the mark and thereby contributed to the perfecting of the written language.

The exclamation mark does its job. In a philosophical book on punctuation, art and politics, Jennifer DeVere Brody used this example to illustrate the power of the exclamation mark: *The hydrogen bomb is history's exclamation point.* In a book from 1892 about literary curiosities, William S. Walsh relates an anecdote about the French author Victor Hugo (1802–85), who had just published *Les Misérables*. Hugo was on holiday, but he was so excited that he sent his publisher a telegram to find out how sales were going. The text of the telegram was concise:

?

The answer he received was both brief and complete:

!

A tired exclamation mark is a question mark.
Stanisław Jerzy Lec (1909–1966),
Polish poet and author of maxims

How Are We Today?

According to legend, the question mark was invented in Egypt or Rome, but we probably have to go to Aachen to find the source. Or should we go to the Middle East?

The question mark is easy to get to grips with; it rarely causes controversy and offers few borderline cases for belief, doubt and pondering over in the small hours. We are dealing with a punctuation mark that gives us writers useful help. All the same, it is said that the question mark is a mere 1,200 years old. Can that be correct? Two myths tell different stories:

- The Ancient Egyptians loved cats. According to the anecdote, one day a man observed his cat looking surprised. Perhaps it was suspicious of something; at any rate, it was perplexed. The man noted that the cat's tail curled into something resembling the modern question mark. He is said to have been so enchanted that he drew the curly tail and began to use it when he wrote questions.
There is no scientific evidence to support this myth.
- Medieval Rome is the scene for another inventive explanation of how the question mark came into existence. The Latin word *quaestio* means question, and the word was probably abbreviated to *qo*, with a variant in which

the *q* was placed above the *o*, creating something that resembles today's *?*.

The story is logical and enticing, but no studies of medieval Roman manuscripts support the theory.

Setting good stories aside, the question mark was another of the innovations introduced by Alcuin, the teacher, monk and minister of information in Charlemagne's empire. Many of those who were to read or edit ancient Latin texts had a different mother tongue. They worked hard and needed all the help and support that punctuation marks could provide. How were they to know whether a sentence was a statement about the world or a question? We know the answer, and for us it can seem surprising that no one had thought about it. But this was around the year 800; the fall of the Roman Empire had resulted in fewer people having the ability to read and write and not many cared about punctuation.

However, Alcuin took the matter in hand. He created *punctus interrogativus* – the exclamation mark. Visually, the new punctuation mark was a combination of a tilde and a full stop, though in some versions the full stop was missing. The mark caught on and was soon used by writers throughout the Carolingian Empire, meaning the whole of central Europe. It made things easier for the increasing number of people who read silently, and it also provided a clear message for those who read the texts aloud.

You are coming now.

The meaning is clear: I am stating that you are coming now.

You are coming now?

The meaning has changed. I am asking whether you are coming now. This is important information for a reader, and if I am going to read the text aloud, I will change the intonation of the sentence as soon as I realise that a question is involved.

In the centuries after its invention the question mark became popular, though it was not always used in accordance with the original idea. It did not acquire its final shape and defined usage until the Venetian Renaissance. In his famous manual of punctuation and typography, *Orthographiae ratio*, published in 1566, Aldo Manuzio the Younger specified that it should be used after questions that required an answer.

The question mark was originally an aid for preachers who needed to know whether they were faced with a statement or a question. If it was a question, they would raise their voice at the end of the sentence, as we also normally do. Later, the question mark was also enclosed in a grammatical framework. It indicates the end of a completed meaning, which in this case is a question.

So the modern question mark is the result of a collaboration between scribes in Aachen and Venice, but could it be that the origin of this punctuation mark is to be found in a completely different place, without having to fall back on amusing myths? Chip Coakley is an expert on manuscripts at the Cambridge University Library in England. In 2011 he identified what may be the world's oldest question mark in a Bible written in Syriac, dating from the fifth century AD. Syriac is a Middle Eastern language that had its golden age before the great expansion of Islam. Coakley told the research journal of Cambridge University that over the years he had become increasingly interested in small elements of the language, such as punctuation.

The Syriac question mark resembles the modern colon: two dots, one above the other. *Zawga elaya*, as the mark is called, is placed above a word near the beginning of the sentence to indicate that it is a question. It is used only when there may be doubt about whether or not the sentence is a question, so not in questions that in English begin with words starting with *wh*.

Could we have managed without the question mark today? Hardly! The question mark is not difficult to deal with. As a rule its use is straightforward – to mark a direct question:

What are you going to knit for your next grandchild?

We also use it when the question is implied:

You'll be knitting something for your next grandchild?

But we cannot use it if the question is indirect; then we use a full stop:

I asked her if she was knitting something for her next grandchild.

Note that we do not put a comma in cases like this:

What are you going to knit for your next grandchild? asked the neighbour.

The question mark is also used after what are known as rhetorical questions, that is, questions where the answer has already been given or where we are not expecting an answer:

Are you stupid?

Note also how the choice of punctuation mark changes the meaning of what you say:

How dare you?
How dare you!

Occasionally we want to put several question marks one after the other, as a way of underlining the profundity of a question. Some people will shake their heads when you do this, so think it over carefully first.

E?? You got an E for the exam?

If you want to emphasise strong feelings still further, you can also combine question marks with an exclamation mark. But here too you should think it over carefully – the border between the serious and the affected can be wafer thin, and this kind of punctuation will make some people wag a warning finger at you.

E?! You got an E for the exam?

In the 1580s the English printer Henry Denham introduced a mark of his own that was to be used after rhetorical questions, *punctus percontativus*.

Are you stupid ⸮

This punctuation mark was never a success. Nor was the *point d'ironie*, introduced by the French poet Alcanter de Brahm in a book of 1899. A number of people both before and after de Brahm have introduced punctuation marks intended to indicate irony or irritation. None of them were successful. We already have both question marks and exclamation marks for this purpose?!

One special use of the question mark is alive and well in Spain. In Spanish they do the same with question marks as with exclamation marks: they put them both before and after the sentence – and the one at the beginning is inverted. The reader is given an indication of what is coming at the very start of the sentence: *¿Donde está tu padre?* (Where is your father?)

A few years ago the television pastor Joel Osteen, known from the American TV network God TV, posted this neat sentence on Twitter: *Never put a question mark where God has put a period.* This tweet was a variation on a 50-year-old quotation from the American comedienne Gracie Allen (1895–1964), who wrote in a letter: *Never place a period where God has placed a comma.* Later, the United Church of Christ added to it in their motto: *Never place a period where God has placed a comma. God Is Still Speaking.*

However, this is a chapter about the question mark, so in this case an American pastor may have the last word: *Where God has put a period, the devil puts a question mark, casting doubt.*

When it comes to punctuation,
You know we're number one.
And to the people of every nation:
Feel the power of the semicolon.
The comedy music group, The Lonely Island

This Punctuation Mark Separates and Unites; it points back to what has been and forward to what is to come

The semicolon has been the cause of a duel in Paris, and also an April Fools' joke that aroused fury. In his book *The Art of the Novel* the author Milan Kundera wrote that he left a publisher who tried to replace his semicolons with commas. The most beautiful of all punctuation marks truly has power over the emotions.

Strictly and objectively considered, we do not need the semicolon. The full stop is absolutely essential. The comma also does an invaluable job for us when we want to put low fences between units of text that do not completely belong together. The colon tells us that something is coming, the question mark indicates that we are wondering about something and the exclamation mark that we are raising our voice. But what about the semicolon? One could live an entire life without using a single semicolon. I also know many professional writers who never have recourse to the semicolon; their texts can be understood, and I have never heard that they are paid less because they do not use the full arsenal of punctuation marks. The American author Kurt Vonnegut said it straight out: 'Do not use semicolons. They are transvestite hermaphrodites representing absolutely nothing. All they do is show you've been to college.'

Vonnegut is far from alone in his hatred of the semicolon. In linguistic debates on the internet in the USA it is asserted that the semicolon is feminine, or alternatively homosexual, and in the English newspaper *The Times*, the columnist Ben Macintyre referred to the unwritten American rule that real men do not use semicolons. Michael S. Reynolds, in his biography of Ernest Hemingway *The Homecoming* (1992), quotes Hemingway thus: *I have to deny myself many small comforts like toilet paper, semicolons and soles to my shoes*. And why did Hemingway deny himself all this? He was worried that the aforementioned goodies might threaten his macho reputation. Animosity towards the semicolon is not exclusively American, but an Irish writer living in the United States believed he had found the answer in what he perceived as a distinctive attitude over there: the Americans have a dislike of nuances and complexity.

But then it nevertheless appears that the semicolon is popular, at any rate in some language communities. In 2012, the Swedish journal *Språktidningen* asked its readers what their favourite punctuation mark was. The semicolon won with 23 per cent of the votes. The full stop and comma only got 13 per cent each.

Are we seeing a new renaissance for the semicolon? It was Aldo Manuzio the Elder who wrote the first modern semicolon and explained that the mark should be used between sentences whose meaning is linked. The first time the semicolon appeared in print was in 1494 in Pietro Bembo's book *De Aetna*. In the years that followed, its shape and use became established practice, first in the print shops of Venice and then gradually in other Italian cities. Supporters of the semicolon are so grateful for Manuzio's innovation that they have made 16 April, the day he died, World Semicolon Day.

The philologist Paul Bruthiaux discovered that the first

semicolon was written in English in 1560 and that 50 years later it appeared in a version of Shakespeare's sonnets. In a short time it had become a winner among punctuation marks. Bruthiaux has investigated the incidence of semicolons – as compared to colons and dashes – in texts written by linguists over five centuries.

- He found that the number of semicolons per 1,000 words rose from 0 in the sixteenth century to 50 in the seventeenth century and 68 in the eighteenth century. That was when it reached its peak.
- In the nineteenth century there were 18 semicolons per 1,000 words and in the twentieth century only 10.
- Also, in comparison with the colon and the dash, the semicolon's position became weaker than in its golden age, falling from total superiority in the eighteenth and nineteenth centuries to being used only to the same extent as the other two in the twentieth century.
- Altogether, the use of the three punctuation marks fell from 93 per 1,000 in the seventeenth century to 25 in the nineteenth century. Over the course of 200 years, dense punctuation was replaced by a plainer, more frugal use of punctuation marks.

Bruthiaux explains the rise and fall of the semicolon by a change in the approach to punctuation. When the semicolon became popular, punctuation was frequently based on syntax, especially among those who wrote grammar text-books. And there were a large number of these. In 1852, the American grammarian Goold Brown investigated how many English grammar books had been written. He counted 548. Heavy punctuation based on grammatical logic was gradually replaced by a rhetorical approach, where punctuation was inserted on the basis of what felt right in terms of pauses. Practice changed from logic to taste, even though grammar books insisted that the earlier rules should be retained. This in itself is proof that our linguistic habits do not necessarily bother about what is prescribed by the writers of grammar books.

Few nations have greater awareness of and admiration for their own language than the French. This love was the basis of the April Fools' joke on the news website Rue89. com in 2008. The newspaper wrote that the president at the time, Nicolas Sarkozy, had issued a decree that all official documents should contain at least three semicolons per page. The joke was a great success. It was not very likely, but not completely incredible. President Sarkozy had often got involved in matters concerning the French language, and a campaign on behalf of the semicolon fitted in well with this. Changes to written French have also been influenced by English. These changes include shorter sentences and fewer punctuation marks. So why could there not be a campaign on behalf of the semicolon from the Élysée Palace?

French feelings about the semicolon were also described in the book *Le Duel. Une passion française*. Among the duels described by the author Jean-Noël Jeanneney is a battle between two university professors in Paris in 1837. One wanted a semicolon in a sentence, the other a colon. As the conflict could not be resolved by a full stop, there was nothing for it but a duel. The semicolon professor was stabbed in the arm, so we may conclude that the semicolon suffered a defeat in this case.

We must therefore not ignore the fact that the losing professor would have been delighted by the research conducted by Cecilia Imberg at the University of Lund almost 200 years later. Her dissertation showed that Swedes in their thirties used many more semicolons than those aged over 50. This may be due to the fact that tastes have changed once again, but it may also be to do with the misuse of the semicolon. In a dissertation from Gävle University College, Alexander Katourgi came to the conclusion that two out of three semicolons in everyday Swedish prose flout the rules. The chief mistake is that the semicolon is used where there should be a colon. Many people write thus:

> *The coach had chosen these players; Anders And, Donald Duck and Kalle Anka.*

Correct punctuation:

> *The coach had chosen these players: Anders And, Donald Duck and Kalle Anka.*

Both the similar look and similar names may be reasons why many people put a semicolon where there should be a colon. But when should we use a semicolon?

1. To separate but link together

The semicolon is used between independent sentences that could also be separated by a full stop. It gives the extra information that what is said in the first sentence is closely connected with what is in the second:

> *Yesterday I wrote a news article; today I'm slaving over a caustic commentary.*

Alternatively, we could have put a full stop:

> *Yesterday I wrote a news article. Today I'm slaving over a caustic commentary.*

In some languages we could also separate the two sentences with a comma without having much to fear:

> *Yesterday I wrote a news article, today I'm slaving over a caustic commentary.*

Those who know the rules of English punctuation will get out their red pens for the comma version; in English, separating two independent sentences with a comma is called a *comma splice*, and it is considered to be one of the gravest comma mistakes of all.

However, in a language like Norwegian it can be acceptable once in a while. The comma signals that the speed is rapid and the pause should be short. The semicolon asks us to make a slightly longer pause, and the full stop an even longer one. What is more, the semicolon tells us that there is a close connection in the content of the two sentences that are both separated and linked by the full stop.

2. Lists

The semicolon can also be used where a comma alone would be confusing:

> *The new committee was as follows: Reidar Jensen, chairman; Kurt Olsen, vice-chairman; Odd Leif Andreassen, treasurer.*

Have a look at this sentence as well:

> *Five seconds before the child looks away, the heart rate speeds up, five seconds after the child has looked away, the heart rate returns to normal.*

There is nothing wrong with this sentence, but it is easier to read and understand with a semicolon:

Five seconds before the child looks away, the heart rate speeds up; five seconds after the child has looked away, the heart rate returns to normal.

Write concisely! That is the advice that is imprinted in you on courses and in books offering you guidance on how to write better. This advice applies as a general rule, but it must be followed in moderation. Long sentences may be hard to work out, but sequences of exclusively short sentences can become intense and tiring to read. The Swedish author Olof Lagercrantz put it brilliantly: 'It all depends on the rhythm. An inner organisation that is difficult to access! The breathing of a language. Thought and rhythm are inseparably united.'

When we write long sentences, the comma is a good friend for carefully separating the parts that are not as closely entwined as two people who have just fallen in love. When we want to show that what we have written has to do with what is coming, it is even better to resort to the semicolon; by doing so we stress the connection and give the text a rhythm with both food for thought and forward thrust.

A sensitively placed semicolon can create clarity in what you write, while at the same time ensuring that the reader is easily carried further on in the text – and, in some cases, it can even add a touch of beauty to the text!

Martin Luther King Jr demonstrated the power of the semicolon in a letter he wrote from jail in Birmingham, Alabama in November 1963. He argued that racial discrimination had to be abolished soon and that there was no point in waiting any longer. He did this in a sentence containing 316 words and nine semicolons. After each semicolon he introduced the next part with *when,* an effective rhetorical device known as *anaphora.*

Find the semicolons in this!

But when you have seen vicious mobs lynch your mothers and fathers at will and drown your sisters and brothers at whim; when you have seen hate filled policemen curse, kick and even kill your black brothers and sisters; when you see the vast majority of your twenty million Negro brothers smothering in an airtight cage of poverty in the midst of an affluent society; when you suddenly find your tongue twisted and your speech stammering as you seek to explain to your six year old daughter why she can't go to the public amusement park that has just been advertised on television, and see tears welling up in her eyes when she is told that Funtown is closed to colored children, and see ominous clouds of inferiority beginning to form in her little mental sky, and see her beginning to distort her personality by developing an unconscious bitterness toward white people; when you have to concoct an answer for a five year old son who is asking: 'Daddy, why do white people treat colored people so mean?'; when you take a cross county drive and find it necessary to sleep night after night in the uncomfortable corners of your automobile because no motel will accept you; when you are humiliated day in and day out by nagging signs reading 'white' and 'colored'; when your first name becomes 'nigger,' your middle name becomes 'boy' (however old you are) and your last name becomes 'John,' and your wife and mother are never given the respected title 'Mrs.'; when you are harried by day and haunted by night by the fact that you are a Negro, living constantly at tiptoe stance, never quite knowing what to expect next, and are plagued with inner fears and outer resentments; when you are forever fighting a degenerating sense of 'nobodiness' – then you will understand why we find it difficult to wait.

I was the type who looked at discussions of What Is Truth only with a view toward correcting the manuscript. If you were to quote 'I am that I am,' for example, I thought that the fundamental problem was where to put the comma, inside the quotation marks or outside.

Umberto Eco

The Comma: A Help and a Hindrance

There is no way round it. I have to begin with a declaration of love:

> The comma creates a breathing space in a life filled with words.
> The comma transforms a chaos of thoughts into an organised
>   sequence of ideas.
> The comma fills you with the power to reach the reader's brain
>   and heart.
> It has been working effectively for those who write since 1494.
> Give the comma a chance.

No punctuation mark causes as much trouble as the comma. When should we put it where, and when should we not put one at all?

Nor does any punctuation mark create as much argument as the comma. And no punctuation mark is better suited to confuse or create peculiar situations if it is left out or used incorrectly. You know the stories? *Let us eat Grandmother.* But let us go back to the beginning:

Eureka! I have found it! This cry is said to originate with the mathematician Archimedes (287–212 BC). He had discovered the law of the buoyancy of bodies in water and he supposedly ran naked through the streets shouting *eureka!* Archimedes was one of the intellectual stars of the library of Alexandria and he collaborated closely with the chief librarian Eratosthenes. So it may well be that Eratosthenes' successors knew the anecdote about Archimedes. At any rate, Aristophanes would have had good reason to shout his own *eureka!* throughout the cultural world of the time. What he had invented was the first system of punctuation, and one of his *distinctiones* was *media distinctio*, which indicates a short pause. Our modern comma had been conceived, though it took its name not from the pause it indicates but from the Greek word *komma*, which means *part of a sentence.*

Unfortunately, Aristophanes' punctuation system fell completely out of use. In the centuries that followed, hints of punctuation appeared here and there, but it was Alcuin and Charlemagne at his residence in Aachen who were responsible for a genuine new advance for the comma. A thousand years had passed since Aristophanes inserted his dots back in Alexandria. Alcuin cut down on punctuation. Several systems had been used during the same periods. *Punctus flexus* had an accent over Aristophanes' comma mark and was used for short pauses within sentences. Later a *punctus elevatus* was used, to some extent in the same way as today's comma. Visually it resembled an inverted semicolon. Professor Boncompagno in Bologna came closest to the modern comma when in the early 1300s he introduced virgula suspensiva:

/

Confused? If so, it is not without reason. The development of the comma was complicated in the 1,700 years after Aristophanes sowed the first seed. It went forwards, backwards and sideways, so the time was definitely ripe for tidying up. The opportunities to print books instead of writing them by hand was a further motive for standardising punctuation.

Then our hero appeared. Aldo Manuzio stated what the

comma should look like and how it should be used. The first time they were used in that way was in Pietro Bembo's *De Aetna* in 1494. In fact, the story could have ended there in Venice over 500 years ago – with a unique success, as the modern comma gradually became standard in Europe. The waves created by this punctuation mark concerned whether it should be used according to rhetorical or grammatical principles. Most language communities take their comma rules from a mixture of these two principles in different proportions. That is why many people perceive the comma rules as impenetrable.

All the same, whatever their ability to punctuate, there is one thing from primary school that few people forget. Because in this case, it was a matter of life and death!

Hang him don't wait until I come.

Where does this school example come from. Who was hanged? The origin has not been fully explained, but might it be based on a true story, presented in a very simplified form for pedagogical reasons? Here are three alternative stories:

Alternative 1: The Irish rebel who was hanged

There is a true story about a man who was hanged after a dispute over the placing of a comma. The man was Roger David Casement (1864–1916), an Irish nationalist, patriot, activist and poet. In April 1916, Casement was arrested by the British police on suspicion of high treason, sabotage and espionage. When the case came to court, the crux of the matter was whether Casement's activity in Germany fell within the scope of the law that the prosecution had found, which was still in force at the time: the medieval Treason Act of 1351.

The defence claimed that the act only applied to crimes committed on British soil, while the prosecution maintained that it also applied if the alleged treasonable act had taken place abroad. The core of the dispute was the claimed appearance of a comma. According to a database of British law, the text reads as follows:

> ... if a Man do levy War against our Lord the King in his Realm, or be adherent to the King's Enemies in his Realm, giving to them Aid and Comfort in the Realm, or elsewhere ...

If the third comma appeared in the original text of the act, treasonable acts committed outside Britain would also fall within the scope of the act, as *elsewhere* would then refer to giving aid and comfort to the king's enemies not only within his realm but also to such activities when carried out on foreign soil.

If the comma did not appear in the original, the accused would go free, because the act would apply only to such activities if they were committed on British soil, not if they were carried out in other places where the king's enemies might be found.

The fact that the original text of the act was in Norman French did not make matters any easier for the court. However, the opinion of the court was that the disputed comma was there and Casement was condemned to death. During the High Court's consideration of the appeal, some said that what might possibly look like a comma in the original French text was only a mark left by the folding of the manuscript. The High Court did not lend much credence to this explanation. The original verdict was upheld.

Roger Casement was hanged in Pentonville Prison in London in August 1916.

Alternative 2: When the Tsarina of Russia intervened

When Princess Dagmar of Denmark married Tsar Alexander III in 1866, she became Tsarina Maria Feodorovna of Russia. The story goes that on one occasion she saved the life of a criminal whom her husband Alexander had decided to send to certain death in Siberia. The Tsar had written: *Reprieve impossible, to be sent to Siberia.* Maria moved the comma so that the sentence became: *Reprieve, impossible to be sent to Siberia.* The man was released.

Alternative 3: The King of Prussia's open decision

In 1873, the typographers in Christiania (an earlier name for the Norwegian capital Oslo) distributed the (handwritten!) trade union journal *Guttenberg.* In it the editor discussed a story about King Frederick the Great of Prussia. Frederick had his own court printing works, with his trusted employee Martin as its head printer. One day, there was a comma missing from a printed resolution and Frederick decided to demonstrate to the head printer how important a comma can be. A political criminal had been condemned to death, but recommended for reprieve. The court asked the king what the final outcome should be. King Frederick seized the opportunity and sent this message to Martin:

Hängt ihn nicht begnadigt.
Friedrich R.
Hang him not reprieved.
Frederick R.

Even a marriage can stand or fall by a comma:

As I was undressing, Mary, my wife, walked into the bedroom.
As I was undressing Mary, my wife walked into the bedroom.

The Danish comma war

The Danes are not generally known for being quarrelsome, but there is one area in which civil war rages: Should there be a comma before a subordinate clause (dependent clause)?

Historically, the Danes followed a German system for the use of commas: Commas should be placed between clauses on the basis of grammatical analysis. In the comma reform of 1918 this system was retained but at the same time rhythmic use of commas was introduced as a valid alternative. The rhythmic-pause comma was intended to be placed where it would be natural to pause when talking. However, this system was very little used.

The grammatical comma has prevailed. In Danish there must always be a comma before a subordinate clause:

Vi forventer, at det bliver regnvejr.
Jeg gik, for at hun kunne være alene.
Spis, så længe du er sulten.

(We expect, that it will rain.
I left, so that she could be alone.
Eat, when you are hungry.)

That is how Danish was supposed to be written until 1996, and it continued to be permissible to write in this way after that date. With the new comma rules that were introduced as a parallel system in 1996, the Danes were given freedom of choice. If you so desire, you no longer have to put what the Danes call a *startkomma* before subordinate clauses that are essential in order for the meaning of the sentence as a whole to be complete. According to the new rules, the sentences above would read like this:

Vi forventer at det bliver regnvejr.
Jeg gik for at hun kunne være alene.
Spis så længe du er sulten.

However, the new rules made people furious and the war has raged almost continuously, even after the Danes changed the rules yet again in 2004. Then a comma system was brought in, but with freedom of choice in one single area. Speakers of the language may choose whether or not they wish to use the *startkomma* before subordinate clauses. The Danish Language Council is in favour of dropping the *startkomma*, but they have few supporters. The teachers have resisted it, journalists and editors likewise, and the Minister of Education has acknowledged that it can cause problems when pupils move from a school that practises the grammatical comma to a school that teaches according to the new rules. Almost everyone has continued to use the old rules, resulting in 40–50 per cent more commas than according to the comma rules that apply in Norwegian, Swedish, Icelandic, English, Dutch, Italian and French.

However, there are some people who choose not to use the *startkomma* before all subordinate clauses. In the Danish newspaper *Kristeligt Dagblad*, Niels Davidsen-Nielsen wrote an article on the commas in the six-volume work *Min Kamp* by the Norwegian author Karl Ove Knausgård. The Danish translator, Sara Koch, had chosen not to use the *startkomma* before all subordinate clauses. The result? For those who prefer the traditional Danish comma rules, there are 37,332 'missing' commas. The total of 37,332 missing commas means 37,332 keystrokes saved, and Davidsen-Nielsen suggests: 'Maybe the publishers could have considered issuing a supplementary volume containing all these commas – free to use.'

The Danes argue about the comma, but maybe the war can be called off. At any rate, that is what Jørn Lund, the chairman of the Danish Language Council, hopes. According to the newspaper *Politiken*, he proposes that the old rules may be used but that, in addition, a new system should be introduced following the pattern of usage in Norway and Sweden. He calls this system the *free comma*, and the intention is to rid Danish texts of superfluous commas, and to meet towards those who do not care about grammatical rules. With the *free comma* there would not have to be a comma before every subordinate clause.

However, there is a long way to go before the Danes get yet another new comma system – and even longer before people start making general use of any new system. Until then, translators of Danish texts in most of Europe can be pleased that they do not have to key in almost half of the extra commas from originals written according to the strictly grammatical Danish comma system.

Viewed from outside it is easy to think that the traditional Danish *startkomma* inhibits flow and understanding when we read, but perhaps it works for those who use it. A study of 2018 came to the conclusion that, since 2014, Danish schoolchildren have got better at inserting commas. When taking comma tests, Danish pupils must indicate whether they use *startkommas*. Most of them do, and examiners' reports from Danish schools support the conclusion of the study – the pupils have improved in the traditional use of commas.

The situation in Germany

The cultural critic Andreas Hock describes the situation in the German language as: *Chaos, Anarchie und Tumult* (Chaos, Anarchy and Tumult). His bestseller, *Bin ich denn der Einzigste hier, wo Deutsch kann?*, takes issue with German spelling reforms. Some will call this confrontation merciless but essential. Others will think that the author is old-fashioned; and he is definitely barking up the wrong tree when he writes that the comma has vanished from German as a result of recent reforms.

As an author, Hock defends the Prussian spelling reform of 1901, and this is what he wants – the rules that remained in place through two world wars, a reconstruction with amazing economic results, a cold war, the reconciliation policy and the fall of the Berlin Wall. Then the philologists began to get moving. They realised that the German language was internationally notorious for orthographic clutter and complicated syntax. Something had to be done!

And they did it. In 1995, a government committee presented a proposal for a spelling reform. From the outside, this did not appear dramatic. The aim was to simplify the rules and adapt them to those of neighbouring languages, for example by greatly restricting the use of the character ß for double S (German 'scharfes S' or Eszett). They also attacked the comma rules and suggested reducing the number of rules from 52 to nine. The changes to the language were approved during a conference in Vienna in 1996, and the idea was that the rules should apply in Germany, Austria and Switzerland from August 1998.

Nearly ten years were to pass before the rules began to apply. There were many vehement protests from politicians, teachers and parents. *Der Spiegel* stepped forward as a mouthpiece for the German writers' crusade against the language reform. This is what the author Hans Magnus Enzensberger said to the magazine about the linguistic vandalism that was going on: 'This so-called reform is of course as necessary as an attack of croup. Only people suffering from obsessive-compulsive neurosis can sit year after year on all kinds of councils and committees, where they swallow and digest taxpayers money to no purpose.'

The spelling reform was implemented in its entirety. The Council for German Orthography, with 40 members from six nations, drew up solutions on which they could reach a compromise. From 1 August 2006 the reform was finally in force.

Historically speaking, German punctuation was based on the grammatical principles that were adopted in 1781. It still is, but changes have been made that are intended to make the use of the comma simpler, clearer and more in agreement with the spoken language. One important change brought about by the new rules is that it is optional to put a comma between main clauses connected by *und, oder, entweder-oder, nicht-noch, beziehungsweise eller weder-noch: Ich fotografierte die Berge, und meine Frau lag in der Sonne.* (and, or, either-or, not-nor, or, neither nor: I photographed the mountains, and my wife lay in the sun.) A comma may be used in such contexts if it helps to make the meaning clearer.

On the other hand, the final reform of 2006 made the use of commas obligatory in other cases, where it had previously been optional. One rule that is likely to please many people who write German is the new paragraph 78 of the German orthography rules: *Oft liegt es im Ermessen des Schreibenden, ob er etwas mit Komma als Zusatz oder Nachtrag kennzeichnen will oder nicht.* (It is often up to the writer's discretion, whether or not he wishes to indicate something as an addition or postscript.)

'The comma has disappeared from German,' say the critics. This is not true. The overall total of comma rules has been reduced to nine, but there are numerous subsections. The booklet on the comma rules still runs to 16 pages of text.

The nonchalant ones

Some people are not bothered about the rules; they put in commas at random. Some of them do it because they do not know any better, and in their texts the use of commas is arbitrary and inconsistent. Others break the rules deliberately – often because they are using the comma's musical potential to emphasise the rhythm of the text and the meaning behind the words.

The Norwegian author Knut Hamsun won the 1916 Nobel Prize for Literature for his masterpiece *Growth of the Soil*, but not because he was good at writing commas; he was not. Hamsun had a somewhat inconsequential and unsystematic attitude to the comma rules, but there were commas in his writings and he was conscious of them. In *Hunger*, he mentions irritating flies that refuse to leave the sheet on which he is writing and 'set their heels against a comma'.

When Hamsun's collected works were reissued a few years ago, changes were made to the punctuation. Commas were removed before necessary subordinate clauses, in particular before clauses beginning with *at* (to) and *som* (who, which, as), where Hamsun put commas in his early books, in accordance with the Danish rules at the time. Tor Guttu, the orthography consultant for the new edition, realised that Hamsun had changed his way of punctuating over the years but never arrived at a logical use of commas, semicolons, full stops and dashes. As a result, the punctuation in the new edition is not so very different from the rather free use we often see in today's fiction.

Hamsun won the Nobel Prize for Literature despite his undecided attitude to the comma. Some people predict that Norway will soon have a new winner, but for the time being Jon Fosse must be content with the Nordic Council Literature Prize. His play *Nokon kjem til å komme* (Someone is Going to

Come) is a masterpiece, but there are definitely no commas on their way. Fosse declares that he is preoccupied with orthography and writes very correctly, but with one exception: the comma rules. He thinks it is great if the publishers standardise his language, but if they want to make him follow the comma rules, he bellows with rage: 'Then it would have to be the same throughout the entire publication. The way I write, the comma has to be rhythmical, not correct,' he says. A collection of essays about his literary work is entitled *Å erstatte lykka med eit komma* (Replacing Happiness With a Comma).

Fosse is the classic defender of rhythmical use of commas. A striking number of interviews with him and discussions about his books contain passages in which the use of commas is a theme in itself. An article from 2009 in the newspaper *Dagbladet* is a typical example. Under the subheading *Komma-krakilsk* (literally: '*Comma-quarrelsome*)' the journalist wrote that Jon Fosse, possibly together with Dag Solstad, must be the worst enemy of the comma-rule police. Later on in the text, Fosse gets the chance to defend himself:

My use of commas is what I use to create the breathing and movement and music I desire, and if people tamper with it, I get quarrelsome and crazy. They can standardise me as much as they like, but leave the commas out of it, they are at the centre of the essence of my creative writing. I use commas according to the rhythm, not the rules.

In 2015, NORLA (Norwegian Literature Abroad) invited entries for an informal competition for foreign translators of Norwegian literature. It was won by Éva Dobos with her contribution 'Om kommaet, musikken og noen grublerier'.

(On the Comma, Music and Some Other Thoughts.) In it she wrote about her agonies and broodings when she had to translate Jon Fosse's novel *Morgon og kveld* (*Morning and Evening*) into Hungarian. In the end she ventured to meet the author in a bar in the centre of Oslo. She had only one question: How on earth am I to use his commas in the Hungarian text? Fosse answered:

> *Don't think so much about commas. You must think that my text is music and the words are notes. Then you must put in punctuation to show the rhythm in the melody. Some must sound weak, almost monotonous. Then the tempo can increase. That is how people think and feel. Commas are the essence of my creative writing. Stand in front of a mirror and read aloud. Then you will hear it.*

What happened to the translator?

> *And it was true. After a lot of lonely performances in front of the bathroom mirror, where I stood and recited and sometimes sang as well, Jon Fosse's commas fell into place. The Hungarian text took off. I felt increasingly drawn to his quiet, repetitive, narrative style, his tenacity and precision, his pianos, crescendos and decrescendos and his musicality. And the strange thing is that when a translator becomes accustomed to Fosse's commas, the way back to punctuation according to the rules is extremely difficult. It seems like playing wrong notes.*

The attitude for which Fosse has become a spokesperson is typical of many people who have a strong, conscious relationship with the language, including its punctuation. Many would probably sign up to the clear message given out by the Danish philosopher Søren Kierkegaard (1813–1855) almost

200 years ago. Kierkegaard began by saying that he allowed himself to be guided and directed in the matter of how words should be spelt, but then came this: 'Punctuation is a different matter; in this I yield to absolutely no one.'

The Swedish writer Nils Ferlin (1898–1961) is said to have lived a bohemian life, but he was a pedant when it came to punctuation. In 1951 he had delivered a poem to the newspaper *Dagens Nyheter*. He slept badly the following night, and in the morning he realised why – there was a comma missing. Ferlin moved heaven and earth to get the mistake corrected, but it was no use. The humiliation was a fact in what our confrères call the 'Great Comma Drama'.

Fosse, Ferlin and Kierkegaard were very deliberate in their use of commas. James Joyce possibly belongs among those whom we would more probably call nonchalant. In 1984, the publisher who issued a new edition of Joyce's masterpiece *Ulysses* was forced to work hard. A clean copy of the manuscript had originally been typed by 20 random typists in their spare time and subjected to the author's handwritten corrections and additions, after which the novel was typeset by hand by 26 French printers in Dijon who did not know a word of English. And the proofreading? Joyce added a further 75,000 words. In addition he was plagued by eye problems that gradually caused him to go blind, and as the manuscript was in a print works in France, the amendments would in any case have to have been made from memory. When the corrected edition was published in 1984, 5,000 errors had been corrected, including 1,000 comma mistakes.

1,000 comma mistakes! There are extenuating circumstances, but the author is nevertheless responsible, so Joyce must be placed in the 'nonchalant' category. He also recommended 'reading with the ears' and allowing the senses to play along. In one of his books he wanted to create an impression of thunder, which he did by writing this collection of sounds that looks rather like the unspaced words of antiquity: *bababadalgharaghtakamminarronnkonnbronntonnerronntuo nnthunntrovarrhiounawnskawntoohoohooardenenthurnuk!*

The Norwegian author Dag Solstad is nonchalant, but also lacking in knowledge. At any rate, that is how he was 50 years ago, if we are to believe a study of his collection of writings, *Svingstol*, from 1967. In this, Solstad makes 50 comma mistakes in 24 pages, as postgraduate student Tove Berg discovered in a comma check. The majority of the mistakes concern breaches of Norwegian comma rule 1: comma between coordinate clauses. For example, Solstad writes: *Moren står bundet til oppvasken og inne i stuen sitter faren og leser avisen.* ('The mother stands tied to the washing-up and in the living room the father sits reading the newspaper.') Berg rejects the idea that the breaches of the rule are due to specific stylistic considerations. In her opinion, they must be ascribed to vacillations in Solstad's attitude to the rules.

In 1953, the philologist Asbjørn Sæteren compared the punctuation in texts by the authors Knut Hamsun, Olav Duun and Tarjei Vesaas. Sæteren found that Vesaas used short sentences with an average of only ten words between each full stop, while Hamsun wrote 18 words between full stops. Duun's style was closer to Hamsun's than Vesaas'. Their styles of writing also left a mark on their use of commas; while Hamsun put an average of 1.1 commas between each full stop, Vesaas managed with 0.4. Sæteren considered the punctuation in the works of the three authors to be important for the rhythm of their texts – a deliberate stylistic device. If a comma is placed where others would not have had any punctuation, the speed is reduced. If a comma is placed where others would have put a full stop, the tempo is increased.

Norwegian comma dispute in the deep web

«Bergen er en vakker by» mener nordmenn flest.
'Bergen is a beautiful city' believe Norwegians mostly.

But where should the comma go in this sentence?

If we write Norwegian, that answer is that the comma should be placed outside the quotation marks:

«Bergen er en vakker by», mener nordmenn flest.

However, not everyone agrees. Some of the people I asked insisted that the comma should be inside the quotation marks.

And in the past the comma should indeed have been placed inside the quotation marks, but in 2004, the Norwegian Language Council established that it should go outside, and this was implemented in 2008. The position of the comma in cases like this is the most important event in the sphere of the Norwegian comma in this millennium. This very fact shows above all that there is little argument about the use of the comma in Norwegian, but there have nevertheless been heated discussions about the matter among translators in a closed discussion forum on the internet, on something called the O-ring. Here we are presumably in what is known as the deep web or the dark web – the place for shady business.

People with a special interest will definitely be able to continue this conversation for many years to come. Writing under the pseudonym Petter Blek, in 2014 the Grand Old Man of Norwegian orthography Professor Finn-Erik Vinje published the book *Punktum, punktum, komma, strek.* (Full Stop, Full Stop, Comma, Dash). The professor devotes 40 pages of it to weighing up the pros and cons: outside or inside?

Vinje's conclusion is clear: the logical answer is for the comma to be placed outside the quotation marks, because the comma is not part of the quotation.

According to Vinje, the comma now has a sensible place after the close of the quotation marks, but the rules of Norwegian orthography are still strange when it comes to the position of the full stop. According to current regulations, the full stop should always be placed before the closing quotation marks, so according to today's rules, this is correct orthography in Norwegian:

«Kongens Person», heter det i Grunnloven, «er hellig.»

If you think this seems illogical, you are welcome to start a debate on the subject. If you prefer to spend your time on something else, that is absolutely fine. It is also possible to join in debates on this subject, even if you are an English-speaker, because there too there is disagreement about where other punctuation marks should be placed in relation to quotation marks. Traditionally, the British want the comma and full stop to be outside the quotation marks, while the Americans want them inside. However, there is considerable inconsistency among users in both language areas.

The author of the book you are currently reading believes that, strictly speaking, the outcome is obvious. There is only one logical answer to the question of where other punctuation marks should be placed in relation to quotation marks. Collins has the perfect explanation in *Improve Your Punctuation*:

> *Punctuation marks (full stops, commas, question and exclamation marks, etc) go inside the final quotation mark if they relate to the quoted words, but outside if they relate to the whole sentence.*

These examples show how you can apply the rule painlessly:

> *Melvyn remarked that Veronica was 'a gossip'.*
> *Louis tried to tell her, 'I think I'm drunk.'*
> *Dr Johnson said that a lexicographer was 'a harmless drudge', yet was himself one.*
> *'Any further delay', she said, 'would result in a lawsuit'.*

Does that look odd? Few people will react if you do it differently. The last of the above examples is taken from an online resource, *The Punctuation Guide*, by the American Jordan Penn. But he puts the commas in a different place:

> *'Any further delay,' she said, 'would result in a lawsuit.'*

The English disease: the Oxford comma

> *I wish to thank my parents, Theresa May and Donald Trump.*

Although few people would believe that the British former prime minister and the president of the United States were your parents, the sentence requires a clarifying comma:

> *I wish to thank my parents, Theresa May, and Donald Trump.*

The comma is motivated by considerations of clarity. So we can use it this way in Norwegian too, even though it conflicts with the comma rules, just as we do in this case:

I have a dog, and a parrot that can talk.

Some people who write English put commas in situations like this, and in addition, they often put a comma before the final item in a list:

I ate cheese, meat, and sausage.
We spent the evening at the cinema, theatre, and nightclub.

Outside the English language community we think the final comma is superfluous. The conjunction *and* links the last two elements together and the comma produces an unnecessary extra pause in reading. People who write English (it seems to be largely Americans) either love or hate this curious punctuation –the Oxford comma or serial comma, as the phenomenon is known. The name is due to the fact that it was first identified in a guide to writing published by Oxford University Press in 1905. Defenders of the Oxford comma even trace the tradition all the way back to our friend Aldo Manuzio and his Aldine Press in sixteenth-century Venice. They also assert that the reason many people no longer use the serial comma is entirely due to the need to save money on printing. Professor Harvey R. Levenson of California Polytechnic State University in the United States says that the publishers of *Webster's Third New International Dictionary* saved 80 pages when they stopped using the Oxford comma. He has been an adviser to many newspaper businesses that wanted to cut costs and, in his experience, deleting the final comma in a list produces valuable savings.

The serial comma reached its peak in the United States in 2017 when the court in Maine upheld milkfloat drivers' claim to overtime totalling 10 million dollars – all because of a missing comma. The employment contract implied that overtime should not be paid for the following tasks:

The canning, processing, preserving, freezing, drying, marketing, storing, packing for shipment or distribution of:
(1) Agricultural produce;
(2) Meat and fish products; and
(3) Perishable foods.

There was no serial comma after *shipment*. The court found that the precise meaning of the contract was therefore unclear and sentenced the employer to make the overtime payments. The case could have been taken to appeal but, according to the *New York Times*, in 2018 the parties agreed on a back payment of five million dollars and the contract was amended and an attempt was made to make it more precise. The commas were removed and an unusual use of semicolons was introduced instead:

The canning; processing; preserving; freezing; drying; marketing; storing; packing for shipment; or distributing of:
(1) Agricultural produce;
(2) Meat and fish products; and
(3) Perishable foods.

But what does research tell us? Karsten Steinhauer is a professor of cognitive neuroscience in Canada. Together with colleagues he investigated how the serial comma affects the brain, including by trying it out on German readers. Steinhauer's conclusion was that the extra comma did not make reading easier, but nor did it do any harm.

However, he agrees that the serial comma can be used where it helps to avoid misunderstandings, as in this classic example:

We have invited strippers, John F. Kennedy and Joseph Stalin.

Stalin is unlikely to have stripped, even though the sentence above might suggest it. Nor was he involved when the comma had people seething with rage in Russia in 1905, though one of his predecessors, Tsar Nicholas II, was. In September 1905 the printers at Ivan Sytin's publishing house in Moscow went on strike. They were demanding to be paid not only for the words but also for the punctuation marks. That was the prelude to what later became known as the 'Comma Strike'. The printers soon won the support of workers in other industries and cities: bakers, railwaymen, lawyers, bank clerks, and even ballet dancers. The effects spread far and wide in what is seen as one of history's most complete general strikes, and Tsar Nicholas II was forced to give the Russian nation its first constitution. And it all began with a comma.

The Comma Rules
So how should the comma be used? The rules are extensive and can lead to nagging doubt. The current comma conventions are historically based on grammatical thinking. Over the years, the principle of the rhetorical, rhythmic pause has also been taken into consideration. The rhythmic and grammatical principles together often produce a good solution, but not always. Which consideration should weigh most heavily when the rhythmic usage conflicts with the grammar? The main rule is that you should write in a way that means the reader can easily understand how you want your

text to be understood. Considerations of clarity overcome all the others.

The comma should set boundaries between elements of content that do not belong very closely together but where the sentence is not yet complete. Consequently, it does not correspond to signs of conclusion such as the full stop, question mark or exclamation mark. You should not put a comma between two clauses that must be read together in order to give the reader the full meaning. Another general principle is that you should put a comma where there would naturally be a short pause in reading.

In *The Punctuation Guide,* Jordan Penn gives rules for the use of commas based on grammatical rules (sentence structure). Here are the most important rules:

Compound sentences

A compound sentence contains two or more independent clauses linked by a coordinating conjunction. Independent clauses are those that can stand alone as complete sentences. The most common coordinating conjunctions are *and, but,* and *or.* In certain cases, *nor, yet, so,* and *for* act as coordinating conjunctions.

Rule: Use a comma before a coordinating conjunction that joins two independent clauses.

She purchased the car, but she declined the extended warranty.

The prime minister's plan seemed quickly and sloppily put together, and the opposition party immediately attacked it.

Simple sentences

A simple sentence contains only one independent clause and no dependent clauses. When a simple sentence contains a conjunction, you might be tempted to insert a comma before the conjunction, as you do with a compound sentence. With a simple sentence, however, the general rule is to omit the comma.

Rule: Do not use a comma before a coordinating conjunction if the sentence contains only one independent clause.

She purchased the car but not the extended warranty.

Are you travelling in first class or in business class?

Complex sentences

A complex sentence contains an independent clause and one or more dependent clauses. A dependent clause, unlike an independent clause, cannot stand on its own as a complete sentence. The conjunctions and prepositions most commonly used to introduce a dependent clause include *if*, *because, while, as, although, since,* and *unless.*

Rule: If the dependent clause comes before the independent clause, separate it with a comma.

If you can't see without your glasses, you shouldn't be driving.

Because of the thunderstorm, our flight has been delayed.

Rule: If the independent clause comes before the dependent clause, omit the comma.

Our flight has been delayed because of the thunderstorm.

Exception to the rule: If the dependent clause is not essential to the meaning of the sentence, it should be set off with a comma.

I cannot agree with his position on that issue, though I don't doubt his sincerity. (Not doubting his sincerity is not the reason I cannot agree with his position; it is merely an additional piece of information.)

Rule: If the dependent clause occurs in the middle of a sentence, use commas if it is non-essential; do not use commas if it is essential.

The guests, who were all close friends of the president, refused to speak about the events that evening.

The guests who arrived more than an hour late were greeted coolly by the host.

Compound-complex sentences

A compound-complex sentence contains two or more independent clauses and at least one dependent clause.

Rule: When a sentence begins with a dependent clause that applies to two independent clauses that follow, insert a comma after the dependent clause, but do not insert a comma between the independent clauses.

If we want this business to work, you need to find suppliers and I need to find buyers.

There are other rules in addition to the grammar-based rules. The most important are:

- Put commas between items in lists.
  At school we learn languages, mathematics and history.
- Put commas around insertions:
  Punctuation, an important part of the written language, is under pressure.
- Put commas around answers, terms of address and exclamations:
  'At last,' he shouted.

Are you still suffering from comma-phobia? Then you can resort to the best comma rule of all: Tidy up your sentences. Use full stops.

Then we must also add that you can count on a decent bonus if you spend the 18–20 minutes it takes to learn the comma rules. The benefits, inspired by Miles Maguire's Comma Project at the University of Wisconsin, can be listed as follows:

1. You will be one in a million – or at least not far off that.
2. It is better than spending the rest of your life in the fog.
3. You will impress your friends – and your teachers, if you have any.
4. You will have a chat-up line that nobody else has: *Will you come home with me and go through the comma rules?*
5. You will get fewer red pen marks in the answers you have handed in.
6. Your editing of other people's texts will attract justified attention.
7. It is not certain that everyone will like you correcting their comma mistakes, but you will find out who your real friends are. They will appreciate your comma perfection.

8. You will always have something to occupy you. If you are bored, you can get out the newspaper and hunt for comma mistakes.

9. And most importantly: your written work will improve. If you put commas in the right places, you will write what you intended to write. Your texts will be easier to read, so there will be a greater chance that your words will be effective.

In a book on factual prose, Professor Johan L. Tønnesson writes about the need to improve communication at all levels of democracy, working life and culture. He believes that this does not concern mainly top politicians' television appearances but rather the thousands of pages of text that are produced every day. He mentions random hyphenation and the use of incomprehensible expressions as examples of areas where improvements are needed, but first of all he writes: 'It is not a matter of indifference if people break the comma rules.'

Some Other Punctuation Marks

The Colon: Here it comes

Aristophanes was already working on the colon, but not in the present-day meaning of the word. When he worked out his punctuation system 2,200 years ago, a dot right down on the line (the same position as today's full stop) was intended to indicate a medium-length pause when the text was being read aloud. This *subdistinctio* would come after a *colon*, which is longer than a *comma* but shorter than a *periode*. So the terms used by Aristophanes refer not to the marks but to units of text of different lengths.

The terms have been retained, but they now mean something quite different. As far as the colon is concerned, its visual appearance is also completely different. The colon has been used in many ways. Today it is a special mark with a clearly defined use: it is to carry the reader's attention forward or further, for example from premise to conclusion or from cause to effect. The colon does not cause any commotion and it is not difficult to use it correctly – as long as you do not confuse it with the semicolon.

The colon can be used for several purposes, for instance, before lists and (in some languages) direct speech, explanations and examples. We use the colon to prepare the reader for the fact that something meaningful is coming. In addition it is great to have it when we do not fancy writing 'namely'. *We have three dogs in the*

*family: Peik, Fant and Mora. Now I only need one thing: ice
cream.*

The problem with the colon is the choice between a small
letter and a capital after a colon. The main rule in English is
to use a small letter. However, most people will think there
are one or two exceptions:

- Initial capital when the colon is followed by a proper name:
  *There was no doubt about who had won the election: Donald
  Trump.*
- Initial capital when the colon is followed by a quotation:
  Donald Trump: No one threatens the US.
- Initial capital when there is more than one main clause
  after the colon:
  *He referred to what had been decided: All states must sign the
  agreement and nothing would happen until that had been done.*

Parentheses

Parentheses (like so many other punctuation marks) probably have their origin in Italian humanism. Coluccio Salutati
(1331–1406) was chancellor of the Republic of Florence. He
had been educated in Bologna (and you have come across
him earlier in the book, because he also improved the exclamation mark). In 2017, the Italian linguist Massimo Arcangeli
wrote that Salutati wrote the first parentheses in 1399 in *De
nobilate legum et medicinae*. This punctuation mark acquired
several names; for example, Erasmus of Rotterdam preferred
the designation *lunulae* (meaning 'little moons'). When Aldo
Manuzio published Bembo's *De Aetna* in 1494, parentheses
were already in place (along with such innovations as the
modern forms of the comma and semicolon).

Parentheses (or brackets) come in many varieties. Here we
will be content with looking at the most common type (which
look like this). The message they convey is that something is

coming that I think belongs here, but you are welcome to skip over it. We put abbreviations, clarifications and explanations in parentheses. We think that the information is less important than what we place between two commas – and much less important than what we put between two dashes.

He shouted loudly (and not without reason) that dinner was ready.

The information that he needed to shout loudly is not very important. So it is given in parenthesis. (It is just an aside.)

In most cases we would prefer commas, because parentheses give a clearer signal to pause. Using many parentheses inhibits flow and forward drive. (And always make the message in parenthesis short, otherwise the reader will lose the main outline.) However, parentheses give us the chance to say two things at the same time. They can work well, but the main rules for writers is still: Say the important things first. Then you say the next thing.

When the parenthesis comes at the end of the sentence, the full stop should come after the closing bracket (as here).

When the parenthesis is a complete independent sentence, the full stop is placed before the closing bracket. (As it is here.)

Em dash and en dash

Em dashes look a little like hyphens, but are longer. The em dash also looks like the *virgula planus* designed by Boncompagno in Bologna around 1300, but his *planus* marked an ending, more or less like the full stop. These characters have nothing in common apart from this visual resemblance.

Our dash is a youthful mark. We use it to separate insertions or to mark a pause where the writer wishes to achieve a greater effect than can be offered by a sensitive comma. The dash emphasises what is to come – something surprising or important. In many cases it is a matter of taste whether we use a dash, a comma or parentheses:

He shouted loudly – and not without reason – that dinner was ready.

The message that the food is served is clear and strong.

He shouted loudly, and not without reason, that dinner was ready.

The message is still clear, but not as forceful as when we use dashes.

Dashes are great for when we want to create an artificial pause and build up tension:

In the wallet he found – a spider.

Precisely because the dash is powerful, it should be used with caution. If we scatter dashes all over our texts, the character will lose its power and what we write will appear slightly mannered or immature. We must not cry wolf until the creature is standing in the doorway.

The en dash is slightly shorter than the em dash, but longer than the hyphen. We use the en dash when we want to indicate times between two dates, years of birth and death in biographies, approximate numbers or quantities, routes between places and distances:

- *23rd September 2014–22nd October 2014*
- *The poet James Joyce (1881–1941)*
- *200–300 people had turned up*
- *You take 10–12 litres of water*
- *The Moss–Fredrikstad bus*
- *2–3 miles further on*

In these cases there is no space before or after the dash.

PART III

A Philosophy for a World in Motion

In his novel *The Hunchback of Notre-Dame* (1831), Victor Hugo wrote about the late Middle Ages in Paris. The triumphal march of book printing has begun, and the archdeacon Claude Frollo is resigned:

> *And opening the window of his cell he pointed out with his finger the immense church of Notre-Dame, which, outlining against the starry sky the black silhouette of its two towers, its stone flanks, its monstrous haunches, seemed an enormous two-headed sphinx, seated in the middle of the city.*
>
> *The archdeacon gazed at the gigantic edifice for some time in silence, then extending his right hand, with a sigh, towards the printed book which lay open on the table, and his left towards Notre-Dame, and turning a sad glance from the book to the church,—'Alas,' he said, 'this will kill that.' (. . .)*
>
> *This will kill that. The book will kill the edifice.*

What Frollo feared was not the book in itself, but that the church's monopoly on the truth, the whole truth and nothing but the truth would crumble. As long as God's word was imparted orally, the clerical establishment had the power and authority to interpret or edit the content. The way in which letters, words and sentences were recited could be important for understanding. Where might pauses emphasise the approved meaning, where should an exclamation be inserted, when was a rhetorical question necessary? Now the texts would be written down and published in printed books so that anyone could read and interpret them. As a result, the clergy lost their monopoly on interpretation. That was what gave Frollo the shivers.

The same fear that struck Claude Frollo has attacked those who think that the written language is being destroyed and perverted in this millennium. Digitisation is now the Big Bad Wolf, and he is a nasty piece of work. We write more and more, but less and less on paper. And with pen or pencil? Rarely. Maybe to a great-aunt at Christmas. The superstar media theorist of the 60s, Marshall McLuhan, has described in detail the revolution resulting from the art of printing. Fifty years ago, McLuhan also predicted the electronic media revolution, and this is often interpreted as a funeral speech for the written word.

That is not how McLuhan should be read, because he said so much more. In 1962 McLuhan wrote in *The Gutenberg Galaxy* that the craft of book printing did not actually change anything about writing itself; the main thing that changed was the tempo, just like when the horse was replaced by motor vehicles. Now we also have aircraft and they travel even faster. It is not a law of nature that digitisation means the beginning of the end for written language, but in order to avoid the demise of the written language, we must manage a tradition of writing that has lasted over 2,000 years in the best possible way. After the fall of the Roman Empire, the ability to communicate in writing suffered a downturn. That may not be the main reason why things went the way they did – downhill – in the early centuries of the Middle Ages, but it is not unreasonable to suppose that there is a connection. Historically speaking, things have gone well with civilisations that have maintained the written language, using, refining and adapting it in order to preserve it.

We are living in a post-modern screen culture. More and more communication in letters, words and sentences is taking place on screens that are growing ever smaller. We used to have telephones with cables coming out of the wall. In the 90s, the cables were cut and we began talking on cordless telephones. Today we talk less and write more on mobiles, tablets or PCs, and soon we will be doing it on our glasses, watches or belts. When we write via the new social media channels, we write almost in the way we talk. The written language has met up with the spoken language and we simply have to recognise this: the classic ideals of written text cannot automatically be fully transferred to the new media channels and genres. This means that when we send text messages, add text to Snapchat photos or write to the family chat group in Messenger in private contexts, it is absolutely fine to use words that are not in the dictionary, tack on the odd emoji and worry a bit less about punctuation than we do when we are writing at work or in school, or for an organisation we are representing.

At the turn of the millennium, Jay David Bolter wrote the book *Writing Space* about computers, hypertext and something he called *remediation of print*. Bolter's key point is that the written language has had to adapt to changes. In the Middle Ages, papyrus was discarded in favour of parchment and then paper. Later, handwritten books were replaced by printed books. And now writing on paper is being supplemented by electronic writing. According to Bolter, each of these shifts is followed by a remediation: the written language adapts to the new medium. Much is retained, but new elements also enter the language. The remediation we see beginning means that the written word is now being imparted in more forms than previously. When our grandparents wrote

100 years ago, there was one standard, which had the official state language (or in Britain the King's English) as its ideal. More recently, new genres and forms of writing have pushed their way forward, some of which represent a renaissance of the way the Ancient Greeks wrote: spoken language written down. We can also see pre-alphabetic ways of writing gaining ground. Where the Semites used picture-like ideograms for writing, we now have a wealth of emojis to choose from. ☺

Writing has traditionally been a planned, structured and formal monologue, whereas talking has (often) been a spontaneous, unstructured, informal dialogue. New genres, media and writing situations have resulted in a hybrid – something that is neither writing nor talking. Chat-writing is both, something halfway between. It happens fast, it happens carelessly, and the text we key in is not meant for posterity, hardly even for tomorrow.

Hurrah for the fact that written language is being used in new contexts! However, at the same time we must remind each other that when we sit at our desks and have to pass on written information in the classic formats, we should still strive to express ourselves in accordance with the ideals we learned at school: logically, coherently, with correct spelling and a style of punctuation that promotes communication. And we should do so whether we are communicating on paper or on screen.

What does being able to write actually involve? Kjell Lars Berge, professor of text linguistics, gives the following answer: *The fundamental rule is to write correctly. For many years people believed that this was something that destroyed pupils' pleasure in writing, so they did not place so much emphasis on it. That was a complete misunderstanding. Grammar and punctuation must be learned at once.*

At once!

The Technology of Thought

This book has described the development of some of the recorded conventions for how language is to be used. Punctuation is an element that was introduced late on, but well, as a powerful driver in the technology of the written language. The Greek origin of the word technology is *techne*, meaning 'art' or 'skill', and in his dialogue *Phaedrus*, Plato calls the alphabet itself a techne. In this book, we take that as a good sign, although Plato himself was very sceptical about written language. He thought that writing would ruin our memory and make us dependent on external aids. That was his view, and it is a criticism of written language that can be recognised in much more recent scepticism concerning calculators and computers.

Written language is a technology of the type that is not to be sneezed at. In *Orality and Literacy*, Walter J. Ong, the Grand Old Man of American literary research, maintained that as a technology, the written language is much more important than both the printing press and the computer, and that no invention has changed human thinking more than written language. Like Ong, the Norwegian professor Anders Johansen stresses the fact that written language is a technology of thought. In his book *Skriv!* (Write!) he praises the magical power of writing as follows:

> *People do not write down or write out their thoughts. All those who have a little experience of writing know that that is not how*

it works. Thoughts occur during the process, as a result of the actual effort of formulating them. What I end up having written is usually completely different from what I had in mind when I decided to start writing. If I have not taken the work too lightly, there is always an amazing amount more: I had no idea I had all that inside me.

Professor Johansen also tells his students: Write out the sentences in full and make a point of ensuring that they are grammatically correct. In his experience, as soon as the students realise that *they cannot write as they talk, they need to take a whole lot of decisions that they were previously able to avoid. Then they discover some logical resources in their own feeling for language: Writing with grammatical consistency is forcing one's thought to be consistent.* Language does not exist for the purpose of grammar; on the contrary, grammar exists for language. And that is how grammar does an important job for written language. Punctuation is an advanced part of the technological software of thought. Written language is not natural, and nor is punctuation. Something as boring as hard work is required in order to learn how punctuation can help to produce clear, flowing and coherent texts.

The consolation is that learning how to use full stops and commas is like learning to cycle or swim. Once we have learned to do it, the ability stays with us for the rest of our lives. If it is a long time since you have swum or put a comma in a sentence, you will feel uncomfortable and rusty to begin with, but after a few practice sessions you will once again be back up to where you were. The rules of grammar are an unconscious part of us. We know the rules – we know how to put sentences together to communicate an opinion effectively. You and I also have within us a feeling for what is good, grammatically correct language. We must take this feeling forward with us, and on the way it can be handy to know that, if grammar exists in our subconscious, it may also be true that the subconscious was formed as a result of our own efforts when we try to make our writing as good as possible – clear, correct and well structured. This is not something the writer of this book has made up in a fit of enthusiasm; the idea actually comes from Freud. Sigmund Freud. He believed that the basis of our self-esteem is created through writing. So, if we are to believe Freud, you are what you write. And then I would like to add on my own account, without the support of Freud: Would you like to read a sloppily written text with flawed logic, spelling mistakes and random, inconsistent punctuation? Those of you who are sceptical about Freud can instead be content with a more moderate conclusion: when you write to people who do not know you, you and the text are of equal importance.

Punctuation In Our Time

The web community, post-modernism, individualism and globalisation: many labels can be attached to our times, but all of them can shed light on our lives as people who write. We write a great many things in the course of one short day, and the variety also applies to punctuation. Here is a day in Anne's writing life:

07.00: Anne gets up and checks her mobile. Answers a Snapchat message. She writes in dialect and ends with an emoji.

08.30–10.30: Anne sits at her computer at work. She starts her working day by writing eight to ten emails. In them she makes an effort to write correctly and with the punctuation she learned at school. In her email to a colleague and good friend she uses slightly less formal language and ends with a selection of positive emojis.

12.00: Lunch! Anne uses her free time to comment on Facebook posts and communicate with friends by text messages or other quick media channels. She writes as if she were chatting, without editing, and she is sparing in her use of both commas and full stops. She is more likely to go for exclamation marks!!!!

14.00–16.00: Anne has to go to a planning meeting. She is taking the minutes, and she does this continuously on her computer. She has found that this is the most efficient way. However, when she gets back to her office, she rewrites, edits and polishes the text and checks carefully that all the punctuation is in place. This is only right and proper. However, the meeting was boring and protracted. All the participants were busy with their mobiles most of the time, except when it was their turn to speak. Anne tried not to, but took a quick look at her messages, and hastily wrote a few chatty answers herself, during the meeting. The language? So-so.

20.00–21.00: Anne is ambitious. She is studying for extra qualifications and writes an essay for the course she is following. The language is precise, clear and logical and uses punctuation that emphasises the message.

23.00: Time for bed! The last thing Anne does before pulling the duvet over her is to chat with friends. The words come thick and fast and are sent off in real time without editorial afterthoughts. There is no punctuation either, and she knows that she will not end the chat with just a full stop and no smiley. She has tried that before. A full stop! The recipient thought Anne was in a bad mood. She does not want that to happen.

Anne's writing day is typical. She has many roles as a writer. There are even more recipients, with varying expectations. She writes in a number of different contexts and genres and communicates via many channels. This has an effect on her language. She has a good command of many ways of writing, choosing them with care and according to the rules, which tells her that the message should be adapted to suit the purpose, target group and context. Consequently, Anne can also handle many punctuation schemes, thereby confirming the results of current research in Britain and Australia. A study from 2014 investigated the connection between incorrect language in text messages among young people and the language the same young people use in classic school situations. The researchers' main conclusion was clear. Incorrect language in text messages must not be misinterpreted as a sign of lack of knowledge about correct language, and young people do not transfer the mistakes from text messages into contexts where correct language is required. The reason for the special text-speak is partly haste, and partly a social expectation of unconventional use of language when young people text each other. A Dutch study of 2016 underlines the fact that schoolchildren know that text-speak is not well received in school. Children are aware of genres and are clear about which writing conventions apply in which contexts. When children write a great deal in text messages and other digital media, they are enjoying themselves and they get used to writing. So the researchers' conclusion is that, if there is a connection between text-speak and writing ability, it is a positive one: the more young people write, the better – even if much of what they write is informal chat.

Does that mean that we can relax, breathe out and take it for granted that our agreed standard for punctuation has a safe future ahead of it? Not necessarily. In an article entitled 'Commas and canaries: the role of punctuation in speech and writing', the American professor of linguistics Naomi S. Baron sketches out three possible directions of development for punctuation in the future. The article takes English punctuation as its starting point, but there is little in it that distinguishes between the European-language communities, so Baron's predictions have wide validity. The background to Baron's use of the canary metaphor is the use of canaries as an early warning system in mines. Caged canaries were taken into the mines and if one died, it was a warning sign of too little oxygen in the tunnels or dangerous gases in the air. Because the birds succumbed more quickly than humans, it gave the men time to get out. There are parallels to be found, Baron argues, in changes in the language. She believes it is hard to document such changes in a simple way, but we can also find sentinel species here. They are called full stop, comma, semicolon and colon. Baron's conclusion is that changes in punctuation indicate changes in the way we communicate.

How will things develop? Here are Baron's three scenarios:

1. The trend will continue

If the current development continues, we will probably use fewer punctuation marks. Punctuation will become lighter. It may also happen that we will put less emphasis on grammar and more on what our inner voice tells us is the kind of punctuation that reflects the way we talk. As sentences get shorter, fewer punctuation marks will be required and many educationists will question grammar-based punctuation. Moreover, verbal and written speech currently fulfil many common functions; Baron sees little difference between sending a brief email and leaving a message on an answerphone or voicemail.

2. There will be a renaissance of grammatical punctuation

A less likely, but possible, outcome is that grammar-based punctuation will strengthen its position, at least when we write in formal contexts. An increasing amount of professional writing in work, school and organisational contexts is moving from paper to the internet, so why would punctuation not be a part of that?

3. Permanent schizophrenia

Perhaps the most likely direction is continued schizophrenia: We want to punctuate partly on the basis of grammatical analysis and partly on what happens when the text is to be read aloud. The latter version may be seen as a renaissance of the rhetorical punctuation of antiquity when texts were to be read aloud, but in our times it is more about inserting punctuation in a way that makes the text appear as if we were talking. Baron believes the future will bring a mixed solution, in which there is not just one kind of punctuation for everything and everyone. She also predicts that the difference between the official versions and the punctuation actually used by speakers of the language will increase.

A Punctuation System for Our Time

The story of written language – and therefore of punctuation – will never come to an end. The language changes as we use it. New technologies like book printing and digital distribution on the web provide guidance and frameworks for how we write. Those of us who are preoccupied with the written language need to remind each other that the development of language cannot be reduced to a simple technological determinism, in which we allow these technologies to decide how we are to write. This is primarily something we must do ourselves.

We write better, faster and more effectively if we use punctuation marks deliberately, consistently and in a way that more or less corresponds to the conventions agreed on by our society. To write is to communicate and, like so many others, the word 'communication' also has its origins in Latin: *communicare*. The word is to do with fellowship, understanding and connections. If we are to communicate well when we write, we cannot all keep to individual private rules for how we are to write words, build up sentences or punctuate. So there is still a need for a few common ground rules for punctuation as well. The more we have in common when we communicate, the better we will understand one another.

Today, everyone who owns a smartphone possesses a means of publication capable of distributing a message that in theory can reach the entire world in seconds. However, we also know that our messages are not necessarily registered, understood and interpreted by recipients in the way we hope and expect. Technology has given every person the potential status of editor, so the struggle for attention has become that much harder. In our time it is easier than ever before to get a word in but more difficult to be heard – not to say listened to. If we wish to be understood, we cannot write according to the post-modernist credo *anything goes*.

Neurolinguistic research confirms what we believe: correct punctuation helps us to understand the writings of others more quickly. In a study from 2018, the American researchers Heggie and Wade-Woolley conclude that punctuation sends the reader a message about how the text is to be read. When we read, we divide the text into units that we think belong together. If the punctuation is conventional, the text rapidly delivers the desired meaning and possible misunderstandings are avoided. The researchers Drury, Baum, Valeriote and Steinhauer summed it up in a similar way in a study from 2016. They measured brain activity during reading in order to find out how the inner voice produced by reading affects the understanding. The results? English-speaking readers rely on the commas when they are trying to understand a text. The same results had previously been found among German and Chinese readers (but not among the Dutch, something the researchers will investigate further in order to find out why). Nevertheless, the main conclusion of the research is clear: when you use commas in the way the reader expects them to be used, your message will get through better and more quickly.

Back in antiquity, Aristophanes was the first to create a system in which the comma, full stop and semicolon would help to promote clearer communication. Later, punctuation had its ups and downs, especially the latter, but in the

Renaissance Aldo Manuzio and like-minded contemporaries succeeded in putting in place a punctuation system that became standard in our western language community. I believe that, as a starting point, we should keep to a standard of this kind when we write formally and professionally. If the boundaries are generous, there is a decent amount of tolerance for personal preferences, fun and wriggle-room within the standard.

Common language codes were one of the driving forces behind the great advances in Europe 500 years ago, with a common punctuation system as one of the foundations. In *The Creative Society,* Lars Tvede wrote that common language codes in particular are an indispensable condition if we in the west continue to desire dynamism and creativity.

In his massive tome *The History and Power of Writing,* the French historian Henri-Jean Martin emphasises the idea that grammar is the mother of all creative disciplines and logic made it possible to shape the rules for the particular logic of writing.

Ernest Hemingway was also among the defenders of conventional punctuation:

> *My attitude toward punctuation is that it ought to be as conventional as possible. (...) You ought to be able to show that you can do it a good deal better than anyone else with the regular tools before you have a license to bring in your own improvements.*

But was Hemingway not one of the foremost writers of the last century? He was, but he nevertheless believed that there might be good grounds for deviating from the principles and rules that apply to punctuation – exactly the same attitude as that of Pablo Picasso: *Learn the rules like a pro, so you can break them like an artist.*

Today we say that we must think outside the box in order to achieve progress. That may be so, but it is also true to say that, where punctuation is concerned, people have been thinking inside the box for 2,000 years, and if we do not know what is inside it, most of us will be on shaky ground if we start inserting punctuation marks at our own discretion wherever we think they fit. Picasso broke the rules, but he had learned his craft thoroughly. The footballer Lionel Messi does unnatural things with the ball, but he has also practised simple basic drills thousands of times. The chess player Magnus Carlsen sometimes chooses moves that seem to be beyond all reason and go against the textbooks, but he too once learned chess from the very beginning. The better we know the principles, the basic rules, the settings my computer calls *default*, the better position we are in to do things with punctuation marks to give the text an extra quality of its own.

Theodor W. Adorno (1903–1969) was a German philosopher, musician and musicologist, and a shrewd sociologist who mercilessly criticised interference on the part of the authorities and other institutions of power. So no one would have raised an eyebrow if he had torn the punctuation rules to pieces and sent them to the happy hunting ground of language. But he did not. On the contrary, in a famous article of 1956 Adorno's starting point was a lovely parallel between music and punctuation:

> *There is no element in which language resembles music more than in the punctuation marks. The comma and the period correspond to the half cadence and the authentic cadence. Exclamation points are like silent cymbal clashes, question marks like musical upbeats, colons dominant seventh chords; and only a person who can perceive the different weights of*

strong and weak phrasings in musical form can really feel the distinction between the comma and the semicolon.

So the musician Adorno also ends up by concluding that rules can be a fruitful basis for punctuation, like an echo against which we can test our choices:

One can sense the difference between a subjective will that brutally demolishes the rules and a tactful sensitivity that allows the rules to echo in the background even where it suspends them.

We have to know the rules if we are to break them – and we should also have a valid reason for doing so. The rules are good suggestions but they cannot always be used regardless. That is why we do not require zero tolerance of deviations from the rules, which is the message in British author Lynne Truss's 2003 book *Eats, Shoots & Leaves*. We can recognise the same basic idea in the work of the German journalist and author Andreas Hock who, in his book *Bin ich denn der Einzigste hier, wo Deutsch kann?* (Am I the Only One Here Who Can Speak German?), makes fun of all the changes in the German language right from its conception. These two authors represent the red pen, the champion of the rules, the police constable who always knows best and never sees that discretion can and should be used. Especially when it comes to punctuation, it is also the case that there will often be uncertainty about what is right or wrong, or about what will function tolerably well and what will enhance the text. The competent writer knows that there are options available, where different punctuation marks will produce different expressions and nuances and create different impressions. In her doctoral thesis on punctuation in three Swedish novels, Alva Dahl concluded that advanced and independent writing ability is closely linked to punctuation that will give both able writers and competent readers the opportunity to exploit the potential of the text and get even more out of it. Dahl believes that in this way punctuation can contribute to greater inter-action between reader and writer – not only by creating borders and connections in the text but also by creating a visual and auditory impression. Here Dahl is formulating a complete understanding, in which punctuation marks are more than just the final icing on the cake. The comma, full stop and other punctuation marks are a part of the raising agent in the cake itself.

Even Ben Jonson writing his *English Grammar* in 1617 came close to the point of balance between grammatical and rhetorical punctuation. His image of the balance was that logical punctuation showed the skeleton and structure of the language, while rhetorical punctuation marked its breathing.

We are approaching a philosophy of punctuation that we should greet with enthusiasm. It can be summarised as follows:

- The most important task of punctuation is to support communication, meaning that the person writing places the marks so that, as far as possible, the recipient will understand the message in the same way as the writer. The punctuation should make it easier, simpler and quicker to read.
- The grammatical system of punctuation ensures that the markings are positioned in such a way that meaningful pieces of text are given logical boundaries and connections.
- The rhetorical system assigns the same tasks to punctua-tion that a speaker must perform when preparing an oral presentation: planning, tone of voice, expression,

gestures, movements, pauses, rhythm, speed and intonation. When we write, these effects are not available to us, but punctuation marks can help to mark, underline, emphasise and moderate, just as the body and voice do in a spoken performance.

- Punctuation is often made up of a mixture of grammatically and rhetorically based norms for what you should do, in proportions that vary from one language community to another. Grammar and rhetoric often produce the same result. When they do not, you have to choose. If you know the rules and are certain of what the punctuation marks can do for you, you will choose the one that provides the best communication, and it will help you if you have a clear understanding of context, purpose, readers and the text itself. It can be formulated thus: There now abideth grammar, rhetoric and good communication, these three. But the greatest of these is good communication, because we must seize the opportunities offered by punctuation marks – reflection from a semi-colon, momentary, gentle reorientation from a comma, wondering from a question mark, expectation from a colon, emotion from an exclamation mark – and the finality of a full stop.

The Ten Commandments
of European Punctuation

Punctuation is and always has been a personal matter.
Malcolm B. Parkes, punctuation historian

The principles of Norwegian punctuation are a good starting point for common European ground rules. The finishing point is far from obvious.

The earliest traditions of European punctuation come from Greece and Italy, with significant contributions from Germany, France and Spain. When you read the history of punctuation as seen from the perspective of London, Cambridge and Oxford, you get the impression that the rules were developed and perfected through the English language. That is sheer exaggeration. Insofar as English-speaking efforts have meant anything for punctuation, it is down to the tenacious efforts of Irish monks to punctuate Latin Bibles 1,200 years ago and the meticulous work of Alcuin of York as minister of information in the Carolingian Empire with its headquarters in modern-day Germany.

What about the Nordic countries? When Aristophanes inserted the first punctuation marks in Alexandria, we had enough to do with keeping warm up here in the Arctic; we had little thought to spare for how high or low dots should be placed next to letters. In fact, we did not yet have a written language. We certainly made a linguistic contribution a few hundred years after the birth of Christ, but unfortunately for the worse. The Langobardi from the north conquered what is now Italy, putting the final nail in the coffin of the Roman Empire, and people's ability to express themselves in writing declined. We who came from the far north of Europe were barbarians, and many centuries passed before the written language got back on the right track.

When punctuation was gradually revitalised around 1,000–1,100 years ago, a small number of educated people in northern Europe had also taught themselves to read and write, but neither runes nor the level of our written language indicate that the intent was for signs that could make the text easy to read. *Kys mik* (kiss me) was the message on one of the oldest runic inscriptions found in Gamlebyen (The Old Town) in Oslo, and that could be understood even without an exclamation mark.

The conclusion below is that Norwegian punctuation may be a pattern and example to be followed by the rest of Europe. We will not get there without convincing the other Europeans that we have something valuable to offer, but if the weather had been better in the English Channel in 1066, we could actually have ordered that Norwegian punctuation should be the European standard, because Norwegian would then have been a world language. So let us enjoy this story in parentheses:

(The circumstances were that the English king, Harold Godwinson, was threatened from both the north and the south. Who would get there first? William was on his way from Normandy but the weather in the English Channel was unsettled, with high winds and waves. He and his forces therefore remained weather-bound on the mainland side. Meanwhile the Norwegian king, Harald Hardrada, arrived from the north and the Vikings met Harold Godwinson at Stamford Bridge. It was a tough battle, which the home team just managed to win.

In the meantime, the weather in the Channel had calmed down and William and his men had an easy journey across to the south coast of England. Harold Godwinson's soldiers were ready in Hastings, but they were weary, and the army was weakened after the battle against the Norwegian Vikings. William had an easy match. He became the Conqueror who ensured that the English language was no longer only a mixture of German, Old Norse and Celtic but absorbed more and more French words and expressions.

If there had been less wind in the English Channel in the autumn of 1066, William would have reached England first. He would have fought against the English king. Whatever the result, the winner would have been exhausted, so Harald Hardrada would have been able to walk it to victory. In that event, good and bad linguistic habits from Old Norse would have become the dominant source of language development in what would have been the Norwegian Empire. Then Europe might also have simply accepted Norwegian punctuation rules.)

As things turned out, we have to come to terms with the fact that Norwegian is among the minor national languages of Europe. Our language developed from Danish, which in turn had German ancestry. So we are stuck with a written language of German origin. Our punctuation was therefore based on logical-grammatical thinking, but these rules have gradually been softened up. Back in 1907, the state established the principle that rhetorical punctuation should be the basis for the comma rules and, over the years, considerations of clarity have gained ground. Norwegian punctuation has been free from major conflicts and, through public committees and regulations from the Norwegian Language Council, which makes the rules for how Norwegian should be written, the written language has acquired a functional punctuation system that offers compromises that preserve the best of different punctuation schemes. In Norway, there is public discussion of what we will live on when the income from oil comes to an end. What will the new oil be? I think Norwegian punctuation would be quite a good alternative.

If Europe has a common language, it is football. Pope John Paul II is said to have put it this way: *Of all the unimportant things in life football is the most important.* But that involves being preoccupied with both football and languages. Some of the wisest things that have been said about languages in Norway come from a Norwegian football manager. Nils Arne Eggen managed Rosenborg BK in their glory days in the twentieth century, with victory over AC Milan in Italy in the Champions League in 1996 being the high point. Eggen, who was also a philologist and teacher, said: 'Languages are not about grammar but about communication.'

This should also be the fundamental ideology when we are carving out the principles and ground rules for punctuation. The most important control question of all will be, 'Do the rules contribute to good communication or not?'

Below are the ten ground rules for punctuation, based on a Norwegian system that functions well. Ten rules are not nearly enough to cover all circumstances and situations that may occur when writing, but they establish and specify principles that can also be used in cases that are not directly covered by the rules.

Full stop
1. Put a full stop when you end a piece of complete information. The full stop shows that the message has been conveyed. There is a need for a pause.

Comma

A comma should be inserted to carefully separate parts of the text that are related but not absolutely linked.

2. Put a comma between coordinate clauses (two main clauses or two subordinate/dependent clauses). Then you show that the two sentences are linked but not glued together. The comma says that you should take a moment's pause when you are reading.

> *Little happened in the days that followed, and spirits fell.*
> *Everyone knew that there were plenty of apples in the garden, and that the fence was in bad condition.*

3. Put a comma when a subordinate/dependent clause comes before a main clause. The subordinate clause cannot stand alone; it needs a main clause in order for the sentence to be complete. This is marked by a comma in writing, with a very short pause when we read.

> *The fact that the English language has its origins in German, cannot be disputed.*

When we have written a comma, we can close the sentence with a full stop.

4. Put a comma after a subordinate/dependent clause that is inserted in a main clause.

> *The first people we met, were soldiers in uniform.*

5. Put a comma before non-essential subordinate/dependent clauses, meaning clauses that provide additional information that does not have to be included in order to make the full

sentence complete. Non-essential subordinate/dependent clauses could have been put in parenthesis. The oral equivalent of this is a very short pause before such subordinate/dependent clauses.

Latin, which for centuries was a world language, has now passed into oblivion.

6. Use commas in lists.

At school we learn languages, mathematics and history.

Question mark
7. Put a question mark instead of a full stop after a question.

When should you put a question mark?

Exclamation mark
8. Put an exclamation mark instead of a full stop when you want to stress what you have written, express surprise, strong emotion or insistence: *Just imagine, Grandmother came to call! Norwegian as a world language. That would have been quite something! Now you must pay attention!*

Common commandments
9. All these rules can be used if they can help you write more clearly, so that your message can be understood better, more quickly or more easily by the reader.
10. In addition, you must use these four and other punctuation marks in the best way possible in order to get your message across. Use them for what they are best at in our traditional way of writing – and preferably in accordance with the conventions that apply in our language community.

Adapt punctuation to the purpose of the text, the recipient and the context. One extreme is a formal letter from your company to the prime minister; the other is a goodnight message to your sweetheart in another part of Europe. *One size does not fit all.*

Bibliography

Arcangeli, Massimo. 2017. *La solitudine del punto esclamativo*. Milan: Il Saggiatore.

Adorno, Theodor W. and Weber Nicholsen, Shierry. 1990. 'Punctuation Marks.' *The Antioch Review*, Vol. 48, No. 3, *Poetry Today*.

Baron, Naomi S. 2001. *Alphabet to Email. How Written English Evolved and Where It's Heading*. Oxon: Routledge.

Baron, Naomi S. 2001. 'Commas and canaries: the role of punctuation in speech and writing.' *Language Sciences*, Vol. 23, No. 1, 15–67.

Baron, Naomi S. 2005. 'The written turn.' *English Language and Linguistics*. Cambridge University Press.

Baron, Naomi S. 2016. *Words Onscreen. The Fate of Reading in a Digital World*. New York: Oxford University Press.

Baum, Shari R.; Itzhak, Inbal; Pauker, Efrat and Steinhauer, Karsten. 2010. 'Effects of Cooperating and Conflicting Prosody in Spoken English Garden Path Sentences: ERP Evidence for the Boundary Deletion Hypothesis.' *Journal of Cognitive Neuroscience*, Vol. 23, No. 10, 2731–2751.

Bech, Kristin. 2016. *Fra englisc til English. Et språk blir til*. Oslo: Pax Forlag.

Beltramini, Guido and Gasparotto, Davide. 2016. *Aldo Manuzio: Renaissance in Venice*. Venice: Marsilio Edition.

Berg, San van den. 1995. 'Marking his Place: Ben Johnson's Punctuation.' *Early Modern Literary Studies* 1.3: 2.1–25.

Berg, Tove. 1975. *En utgreiing om prinsipper for kommatering og en oversikt over den faktiske bruken i nåtidsnorsk.* Oslo: University of Oslo.

Berg Eriksen, Trond. 1987. *Budbringerens overtak.* Oslo: Universitetsforlaget.

Blek, Petter. 2014. *Punktum, punktum, komma, strek.* Oslo: Riksmålsforbundet.

Bolter, Jay David. 2001. *Writing Space: Computers, Hypertext and the Remediation of Print.* London: Lawrence Erlbaum Associates.

Bos, Ken van den; Ham, Jaap; Lind, E. Allan; Simonis, Marieke; Essen, Wiljo J. van and Rijpkema, Mark. 2008. 'Justice and the human alarm system: The impact of exclamation points and flashing lights on the justice judgement process.' *Journal of Experimental Social Psychology,* 44: 201–219.

Brody, Jennifer DeVere. 2008. *Punctuation: Art, Politics, and Play.* London: Duke University Press.

Brufani, Stefano and Capaccioni. 2016. *Trevi Culla del Libro.* Trevi: Complesso Museale di San Francesco.

Bruthiaux, Paul. 1995. 'The Rise and Fall of the Semicolon: English Punctuation Theory and English Teaching Practice.' *Applied Linguistics,* Vol. 16, No. 1, Oxford University Press.

Burton, Nina. 2018. Gutenberggalaxens Nova. Stockholm: Albert Bonnier Förlag.

Caprona, Yann de. 2013. *Norsk etymologisk ordbok.* Oslo: Kagge Forlag.

Castells, Manuel. 2000. *The Rise of the Network Society.* Oslo: Blackwell Publishers.

Chartier, Roger. 1993. *A History of Private Life, vol. 3: Passions of the Renaissance.* Cambridge, MA: Harvard University Press.

Collins. 2009. *Improve Your Punctuation*. Glasgow. HarperCollins Publishers.

Crosby, Alfred W. 1997. *The Measure of Reality: Quantification in Western Europe, 1250–1600*. New York: Cambridge University Press.

Crystal, David. 2015. *Making a Point: The Persnickety Story of English Punctuation*. New York: St Martin's Press.

Dahl, Alva. 2015. 'I skriftens gränstrakter. Interpunktionens funktioner i tre samtida svenska romaner.' Uppsala: Uppsala University.

de Mauro, Tullio. 2017. *Prima lezione sul linguaggio*. Milan: Corriere della sera.

Derrida, Jacques. 1976. *Of Grammatology*. Baltimore/London: The Johns Hopkins University Press.

van Dijk, CN; van Witteloostuijn, M.; Vasi, N.; Avrutin, S. and Blom, E. 2016. 'The Influence of Texting Language on Grammar and Executive Functions in Primary School Children.' *PLOS ONE*, Vol. 11, No. 3.

Dobos, Éva. 2015. *Om kommaet, musikken og noen grublerier*. http://oversetterforeningen.no/norge-sett-utenfra-1-premie/

Drury, John E.; Baum, Shari R.; Valeriote, Hope and Steinhauer, Karsten. 2016. 'Punctuation and Implicit Prosody in Silent Reading: An ERP Study Investigating English Garden-Path Sentences'. *Front. Psychol.* 7:1375.

Dunbar, Robin. 2004. *Grooming, Gossip and the Evolution of Language*. London: Faber and Faber.

Eisenstein, Elizabeth L. 2005. *The Printing Revolution in Early Modern Europe*. New York: Cambridge University Press.

Forster, E.M. 2014. *Alexandria. A History and a Guide*. Cairo: The American University in Cairo Press.

Friederici, Angela D. and Steinhauer, Karsten. 2001. 'Prosodic Boundaries, Comma Rules, and Brain Responses: The

Closure Positive Shift in ERPs as a Universal Marker for Prosodic Phrasing in Listeners and Readers.' *Journal of Psycholinguistic Research*, Springer US.

Ganz, David. 2008. *Book Production in the Carolingian Empire and the Spread of Caroline Minuscule*. Cambridge: Cambridge University Press.

Gilliard, Frank D. 1993. 'More Silent Reading in Antiquity: Non Omne Verbum Sonabat.' *Journal of Biblical Literature*, Vol. 112, No. 4.

Gundersen, Dag (ed.). 2001. *Språkvett. Skriveregler, grammatikk og språklige råd fra a til å*. Oslo: Kunnskapsforlaget.

Gunraj, D.N.; Drumm-Hewitt, A.M.; Dashow, E.M. and Upadhyay, S.S.N. 2015. 'Texting insincerely. The role of the period in text messaging.' *Computers in Human Behavior*.

Hancock, Jeffrey T.; Landrigan, Christopher and Silver, Courtney. 2007. 'Expressing Emotion in Text-based Communication.' CHI 2007 *Proceedings of Emotion & Empathy*.

Harari, Yuval Noah. 2011. *Sapiens*. Eiksmarka: Bazar Forlag. English translation by Purcell and Watzman published by Harvill Secker, London, 2014.

Heggie, Lindsay and Wade-Woolley, Lesly. 2018. 'Prosodic awareness and punctuation ability in adult readers.' *Reading Psychology*, Vol. 39, No. 2, 188–215.

Hock, Andreas. 2015. *Bin ich den der Einzigste hier, wo Deutsch kann? Über den Niedergang unserer Sprache*. Munich: Riva Verlag.

Houghton, Kenneth J.; Klin, Celia M. and Upadhyay, Sri Siddhi N. 2017. 'Punctuation in text messages may convey abruptness. Period.' *Computers in Human Behavior*.

Houston, Keith. 2013. *Shady Characters. The Secret Life of Punctuation, Symbols & Other Typographical Marks*. New York/London: W.W. Norton & Company.

Hugo, Victor. 1954. *Ringeren fra Notre Dame*. Oslo: Ansgar forlag.

Hwang, Hyekyung and Steinhauer, Karsten. 2011. 'Phrase Length Matters: The Interplay between Implicit Prosody and Syntax in Korean "Garden Path" Sentences.' *Journal of Cognitive Neuroscience*.

Imberg, Cecilia. 2014. 'Semikolon – utrotningshotat eller bara missbrukat?' Lund: Lund University.

Johansen, Anders. 2009. *Skriv! Håndverk i sakprosa*. Oslo: Spartacus forlag.

Johansen, Anders (ed.). 2012. *Kunnskapens språk. Skrivearbeid som forskningsmetode*. Oslo: Scandinavian Academic Press/ Spartacus forlag.

Joseph, Miriam. 2002. *The Trivium: the Liberal Arts of Logic, Grammar, and Rhetoric*. Philadelphia: Paul Dry Books.

Kaiser, Maria Regina. 2014. *Karl der Grosse und der Feldzug der Weisheit*. Würzburg: Arena Verlag.

Katourgi, Alexander. 2014. *Favoritskiljetecknet. Bruk og missbruk av semikolon*. Gävle: University of Gävle.

Kemp, Nenagh; Wood, Clare and Waldron, Sam. 2014. 'do i know its wrong: children's and adults' use of unconventional grammar in text messaging.' Springer.

King, Graham. 2009. *Improve Your Punctuation*. Glasgow: HarperCollins Publishers.

King, Stephen. 2000: *On Writing*. New York: Scribner.

Lagercrantz, Olof. 2000. *Om kunsten å lese og skrive*. Oslo: Bokvennen.

Loodts, Fabienne and Petermann, Saskia. 2014. *Karl der Grosse*. Aachen: wesentlich. verlag.

Lundeby, Einar and Torvik, Ingvald. 1961. *Språket vårt gjennom tidene*. Oslo: Gyldendal.

Macleod, Roy (ed.). 2002. *The Library of Alexandria*. Cairo: The American University in Cairo Press.

Magris, Claudio. 1999. *Mikrokosmos*. Oslo: Cappelen.

Manguel, Alberto. 1996. *A History of Reading*. New York: Viking.

Marcolongo, Andrea. 2016. *La lingua geniale. 9 ragioni per amare il Greco*. Bari/Rome: Gius. Laterza & Figli.

Martin, Henri-Jean.1994. *The History and Power of Writing*. Chicago/London: The University of Chicago Press.

McLuhan, Marshall. 1968. *Mennesket og media*. Oslo: Gyldendal.

McLuhan, Marshall. 2011. *The Gutenberg Galaxy*. Toronto: University of Toronto Press.

Michalsen, Bård Borch. 2014. *Komma. Kommategnets personlighet, historie og regler*. Oslo: Juritzen.

Michalsen, Bård Borch. 2017. *Skriv bedre!* Oslo: Spartacus.

Moorehead, Alan. 1958. *The Russian Revolution*. New York: Harper.

Ong, Walter J. 2012. *Orality and Literacy: The Technologizing of the Word*. (30th anniversary edition with additional chapters by John Hartley.) London/New York: Routledge.

Pacilli, Mattia. 2009. *Aldo o Il sogno di un Piccolo Libro*. Bassiano: Accademia di vicinato/Amici di Bassiano e d'Europa in cerchio.

Parkes, Malcolm B. 1993. *Pause and Effect: An Introduction to the History of Punctuation in the West*. Los Angeles: University of California Press.

Penn, Jordan. *The Punctuation Guide*. www.thepunctuation guide.com.

Pinker, Steven. 2014. *The Sense of Style: the Thinking Person's Guide to Writing in the 21st Century*. New York: Viking.

Pohle, Frank. 2014. *Karl Charlemagne der Grosse. Orte der Macht*. Dresden: Sandstein Verlag.

Ravitch, Diane (ed.). 1992. *The Democracy Reader*. New York: HarperCollins Publishers.

Reamer, Andrew. 2014. *The Impact of Technological Invention on Economic Growth – A Review of the Literature.* Washington DC: The George Washington Institute of Public Policy.

Sæteren, Asbjørn. 1953. *En dikter og hans stil.* Oslo: Olaf Norlis forlag.

Schildgen, Brenda Deen. 1997. *The Rhetoric Canon.* Detroit: Wayne State University Press.

Skår, Astrid (ed.). 2003. *Sitatboka.* Oslo: Kagge Forlag.

Steinhauer, Karsten. 2003. 'Electrophysiological correlates of prosody and punctuation.' *Brain and Language,* Vol. 86, 142–164.

Strömquist, Siv. 2013. *Skiljeteckensboken.* Stockholm: Morfem.

Thrax, Dionysios. 1874. *The Grammar of Dionysios Thrax.* Hentet fra University of Toronto Library: https://archive.org/dctails/grammarofdionysi00dionuoft.

Toner, Anne. 2015. *Ellipsis in English Literature.* Cambridge: Cambridge University Press.

Torre, Gian Carlo (ed.). 2015. *Aldo Manuzio dal folio al tascabile.* Bassiano: Il Levante Libreria Editrice.

Truss, Lynne. 2006. *Eats, Shoots & Leaves: The Zero Tolerance Approach to Punctuation.* New York: Gotham Books.

Tvede, Lars. 2013. *Det kreative samfund. Hvordan Vesten vinder fremtiden.* København: Gyldendal Business.

Twain, Mark. 1897. 'How to tell a story.' https://www.gutenberg.org/files/3250/3250-h/3250-h.htm.

Vacalebre, Natale. 2016. *Festina lente. Un percorso virtuale tra le edizioni aldine della Biblioteca Trivulziana di Milano.* Milano: Università Cattolica.

Vinje, Finn-Erik. 2011. *Skriveregler, niende utgave.* Oslo: Aschehoug.

Waseleski, Carol. 2006. 'Gender and the Use of Exclamation Points in Computer-Mediated Communication: An

Analysis of Exclamations Posted to Two Electronic Discussion Lists.' *Journal of Computer-Mediated Communication,* Vol. 11, 1012–1024.

Watson, Cecelia. 2012. 'Points of Contention: Rethinking the Past, Present and Future of Punctuation.' *Critical Inquiry,* Vol. 38, No. 3, The University of Chicago Press.

Webb, Stephen. 2018. *Clash of Symbols. A Ride Through the Riches of Glyphs.* Cham: Springer.

Encyclopædia Britannica Online, Store Norske Leksikon, Wikipedia and other common websites.